BY TRAM FROM DUDLEY

PAUL COLLINS

The History Press

First published 2013

The History Press
The Mill, Brimscombe Port
Stroud, Gloucestershire, GL5 2QG
www.thehistorypress.co.uk

British Library Cataloguing in Publication Data.
A catalogue record for this book is available from the British Library.

ISBN 978 0 7524 9316 9

Typesetting and origination by The History Press
Printed in Great Britain

Contents

Acknowledgements   4

The Black Country Society   5

Introduction   6

1   Steam Trams and Electrification   11

2   Dudley to Stourbridge   24

3   Dudley (Stafford Street) to Dudley (Wolverhampton Street)   52

4   Dudley to Cradley Heath via Netherton   54

5   Dudley to Kingswinford via Pensnett   66

6   Kingswinford to Stourbridge via Wordsley   74

7   The Kinver Light Railway   82

8   The Stourbridge High Street Extension   91

9   Stourbridge to The Lye & The Hayes   114

10   Stourbridge to Wollaston via Enville Street   123

11   Old Hill to Blackheath   129

12   Closure and After   134

ACKNOWLEDGEMENTS

I am extremely grateful to the following individuals and organisations, without whose kind assistance and generosity this book would not have been possible: Black Country History in Photographs (www.blackcountrygob.com/Photogallery); Janet Bayard-Jones; June Collins; Taisia Collins; Ray Cresswell and Brierley Printing; Digital Photographic Images (www.digital-photographic-images.co.uk); Peter Glews; Mellanie Hartland; the History of Wollaston (Group); Colin MacDonald (www.stourbridge.com); Val Ross, Laura Waters and Glynn Wilton and the National Tramway Museum; David Postle and Kidderminster Railway Museum; Katie Soley, and Juanita Hall and all at The History Press.

A Note on the Photographs

The photographs in this book have been obtained from a variety of sources. Those obtained directly from the original photographer or a picture library have been duly acknowledged, but some may have been acquired on the open market and, despite attempts at tracing their origin, many of these inevitably remain anonymous. Such photographs are usually credited to the 'collection' of the contributor. Ownership of a print of a photograph, or a copy of a postcard, does not confer copyright upon the owner. In such instances, copyright rests with the original photographer, the company for whom the image was taken, or the person, organisation or company to whom copyright has been assigned. Again, such photographs are usually credited to the 'collection' of the contributor. If, through no fault of my own, photographs or images have been used without due credit or acknowledgement, then apologies are offered. If anyone believes this to be the case, please let me know and the necessary credit will be added at the earliest opportunity.

THE BLACK COUNTRY SOCIETY

This voluntary society of some 1,800 members worldwide and associated with the British Association for Local History (BALH), was founded in 1967 as a reaction to the trend of the late 1950s and early 1960s to amalgamate local authorities and other bodies into larger units and, in the Midlands, to sweep away the area's industrial heritage in the process.

The general aim of the Society is to create interest in the past, present and future of the Black Country. It campaigned for the establishment of an industrial museum. In 1975, the Black Country Museum was established on 26 acres of derelict land adjoining Dudley Castle grounds. This has been developed into an award-winning museum attracting over 250,000 annually.

All members receive a copy of the quarterly magazine, *The Blackcountryman*, over 160 issues of which have been published. In these magazines are some 3,500 authoritative articles on all aspects of the Black Country by historians, teachers, researchers, students, subject experts and ordinary folk with an extraordinary story to tell. The whole represents a unique resource about the area, a mine of information for students and researchers who frequently refer to it. Two thousand copies are printed. Contributors do not receive payment for their articles.

www.blackcountrysociety.co.uk
editor@blackcountrysociety.co.uk
PO Box 71, Kingswinford, DY6 9YN

INTRODUCTION

This book covers the Dudley, Stourbridge & District Electric Traction Company Limited's (DS&DET) tramlines and routes from Dudley to Stourbridge, Cradley Heath, Kingswinford, Kinver, The Lye, Wollaston, Old Hill and Blackheath, which were all constructed and opened between 1899 and 1904. This tramway system operated at its fullest extent for just under twenty-five years and all of the lines closed progressively between the end of 1925 and 1930.

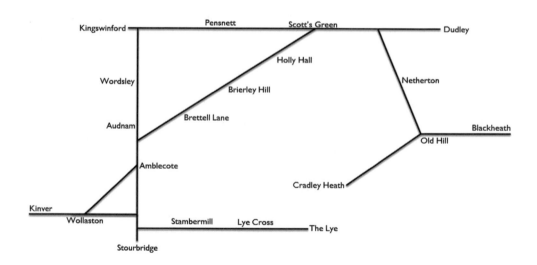

A map of the DS&DET's tramway system, showing the principal places served.

The majority of the places served by the DS&DET's trams could be reached directly from Dudley without the need to change cars. However, the lines between Kingswinford and Stourbridge, Amblecote and Kinver, and Stourbridge and Wollaston did require one change at the first-named place.

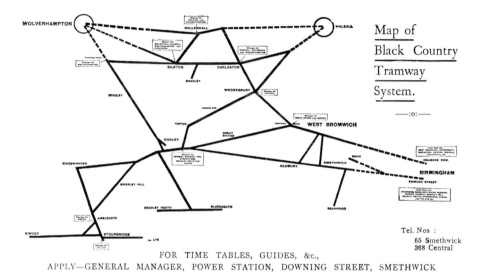

An original map of the Black Country Tramway System, showing all of the places accessible by tram by changing cars at Dudley and in other places. *(Author's Collection)*

These destinations were but a few of those accessible by tram from Dudley. There the DS&DET's lines were physically connected to those of Birmingham Corporation, the South Staffordshire Tramways Co. and the Wolverhampton District Electric Tramways Ltd, creating a greater Black Country Tramway System.

With the exception of the lines of Birmingham Corporation, the Black Country tramways were operated by companies which were subsidiaries of the British Electric Traction Co. Ltd (BET), which had been formed in 1896 with the object of developing electric tramways throughout the country. In May 1904, the managers of the various Black Country tramway companies formed a joint body called the Birmingham & Midland Tramways Joint Committee to control the operation of their companies within the overall BET concern. One major outcome of this was the construction and opening of new central workshops, known as 'Tividale Works', which the Joint Committee built on the Tividale Estate. These were brought into service in January 1907, from which time all major repairs and repaints were carried out there instead of at Hart's Hill Depot, where minor repairs and adjustments continued to be made.

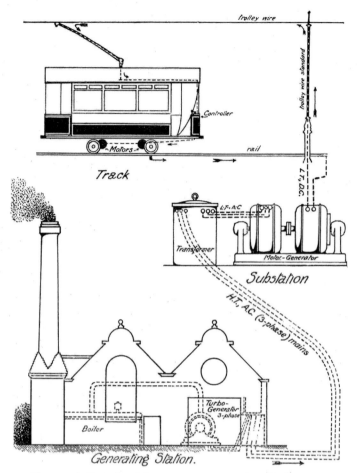

Diagrammatic illustration of the general arrangement of an electric tramway on the overhead system. At the foot is shown the generating station which supplies alternating current at high-pressure (for economy in transmission) to a substation where it is 'transformed' to low pressure and 'converted' in a motor-generator to continuous current for distribution to the trolley wire from which each car takes its current. The course of the current through the trolley pole and controller and thence to the motors and back by the rails is indicated by arrows.

A diagrammatic illustration of how an electric tramway works, which is contemporary to the construction and opening of the DS&DET's lines. (Author's Collection)

Electric trams draw their power – known as current – from copper wires suspended above the running lines, known as trolley wires – or just as overhead. These wires are hung or suspended from cast-iron poles – known as traction poles – either mounted in the pavement or in the middle of sections of double track. From the traction poles the overhead is either suspended from a wire running between opposing traction poles – called span wires – or from tubular arms extending out from near the top of a traction pole – called side arms.

The power is Direct Current (DC) at 500 volts. Being DC the polarity of the current does not change so the positive is fed into the overhead wires and the negative – or return – is via the running lines. Therefore an electric tramway is an electric circuit with a gap in it – one bridged by the tramcar. As the diagram shows, the tramcar's trolley head, mounted on the tip of its trolley pole, makes contact with the overhead and draws the power which passes via the controller, which the driver or Motorman operates. In essence, this is a series of electrical resistances that are progressively switched out allowing more and more power to pass to the electric motors which drive the tramcar's wheels. The current is fed to the overhead wires along feeder cables, which are generally buried beneath the pavements of the roads along which the tramcars run. Power is fed into the overhead at intervals of roughly every half mile. At these points – known as section breaks – both the overhead and the track return circuits are routed through switches housed in a pavement-mounted cast-iron cabinet called a switch pillar. In this way a section of the tramway's line or overhead in which there is a problem can be isolated without the need to close the entire system down.

Some Black Country Tramway Basics

All of the Black Country electric tramways were built using track at a gauge of 3ft 6in (1,067mm). As this width is less than the UK standard railway gauge of 4ft 8½in (1,435mm), the tramways were classed as being 'narrow gauge'. The lines were laid along the main roads which linked the places in question. As constructed, the lines were single – one track – which branched out into short sections of double track at intervals of every few hundred yards. Known as passing loops, these allowed cars travelling in opposite directions to pass one another. Entry and exit from a passing loop was controlled by points in the track which the Conductor operated with a point lever. Above the lines there were separate overhead wires for each direction of travel, usually spaced quite close to each other.

The tramcars – or cars – used on the DS&DET's lines were either single- or double-deckers. The former could seat between 28, 40 and 52-56 depending upon their length. Double-deckers generally seated more passengers – between 48 and 64 – typically with four or so more on the upper deck, but not in every case. The ends of the cars were identical. On the lower deck the ends were called platforms, and entry and exit from all cars was by means of the rear platform; the Motorman occupying the front one. On upper decks the ends were called balconies.

Each car had a crew of two – a driver or Motorman and a Conductor. The latter had many duties, including issuing tickets and collecting fares,

9

operating points, signalling to the driver when the car needed to stop, reversing the car's trolley pole and upper deck seating at termini and calling out the names of the stops to the passengers as each one was approached. Each line had a series of stops. Some of these were Compulsory – where the car had to stop irrespective of whether any passengers wanted to alight or board – and Request – where the car stopped if needed. There were also a number of places on each line where the Board of Trade Inspectorate had determined that cars must be brought to a halt before proceeding. These were typically at the top or foot of hills and busy road junctions. Often or not stops were by or close to readily identifiable places, prominent buildings like town halls, churches or – very often – pubs. The routes were divided into Fare Stages and the fares charged depended upon how many of these were to be travelled.

This book began as a one of a series of illustrated talks I put together just over twenty years ago. In delivering this over the intervening years I have been very fortunate in being loaned or given many postcards and photographs which I have copied or kept. These have formed the basis of the images reproduced here.

Each chapter takes the form of a recreation of a ride along each of the DS&DET's lines using historic images, not all of which show tramcars, but are intended to give an impression of what as a passenger on a tram you would have seen. Each line is illustrated by a map. These have been produced using notes made by Alec Jenson who, as a teenager in the mid-1910s, rode all the DS&DET's lines and made copious notes on them, including sketch maps. One thing Alec did was to record the names of the stops which the Conductors called out – some of which were not exactly their proper ones. How else would we have known that for the Church of St Augustine at Holly Hall, it was common for 'Avanger' to be called out?

Over the years, it has also been a privilege to share the recollections of many people who knew and rode on the DS&DET's trams; most recently Albert Taylor who, aged 102, has a memory which pares the intervening years away and makes it as though you were there.

Each line is also described in terms of the land and townscapes passed through. These have been produced by consulting historic mapping contemporary to the opening of each line.

Paul Collins, 2013

I

STEAM TRAMS AND ELECTRIFICATION

The Dudley & Stourbridge Steam Tramway Co. Ltd

The Dudley, Stourbridge & Kingswinford Tramways Co. Ltd was registered on 22 December 1880 and obtained most of its necessary Parliamentary Powers in 1881. Missing was one line proposed to Kingswinford and to reflect this, sometime in 1882, before construction commenced, the company changed its name to the Dudley & Stourbridge Steam Tramway (D&SST) Co. Ltd. The route followed the main roads between the two towns, commencing in Market Place, Dudley, and going via High Street, (Upper) High Street, Queen's Cross, Stourbridge Road, Dudley Road, Brierley Hill High Street, Church Street, Brettell Lane and High Street to the Amblecote side of the River Stour in Stourbridge. Also in 1882, through failure on the part of the promoters of another steam tramway to comply with the terms of their powers, the D&SST acquired the right to run from Dudley Market Place, down Castle Hill to Dudley Station and there to join up with other tramways at the junction with Tipton Road.

The line was very hilly, there being a difference in levels between Dudley and Stourbridge of 500ft! The gauge was 3ft 6in and the depot was at the top of Tipton Road adjacent to the L&NWR side of Dudley railway station. Construction began in 1883 and was completed by May 1884, a trial run along the line being made in the middle of that month. The tramway was inspected by Major-General Hutchinson from the Board of Trade on 27 May 1884 and opened from Dudley Market Place to Stourbridge on 31 May 1884; the line being extended the short distance to Mill Street, Stourbridge on 30 July 1887.

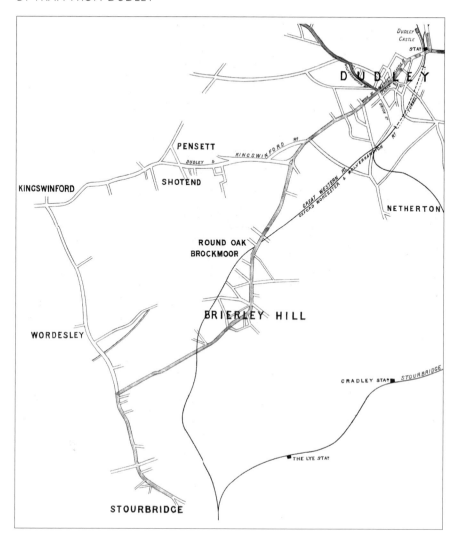

The D&SST's route between Dudley and Stourbridge is shown shaded on this extract from *Duncan's Map of Tramways of South Staffordshire* which was published in 1885 – a year after the steam tramway opened. The misspellings of PENSETT (Pensnett), SHOTEND (Shutt End), and WORDESLEY (Wordsley) are amusing, but at least they called it THE LYE! *(Author's Collection)*

The system employed twelve locomotives and eight passenger cars. These operated from Dudley every thirty minutes between 07.30 and 21.30, and from Stourbridge every thirty minutes between 08.40 and 22.40.

The journey took an hour and the fare was 4*d*, which undercut the train fare for the same journey by 2*d*. Consequently the trams were very popular. Each of the passenger cars seated 62–30 inside and 32 outside (on top). The lower saloon had bench seats with their backs to the windows; the top deck seating was of the 'knifeboard' kind, bench seats arranged with their backs together along the 'spine' of the car, facing outwards. Whilst the lower saloon was glazed and enclosed – even having curtains – the top deck was open-sided with a canvas roof and modest glazed ends which wrapped around the top of the stairs. Entry and exit was by means of the passenger car's rear platform.

A Dudley–Stourbridge steam tram at Dudley Station, c. 1885. The locomotive is No. 3, built by Kitson & Co. of Leeds in 1883. Its number is painted on a valance which shielded the locomotive's drive and valve gear from becoming entangled with stray dogs and the hems of ladies' long dresses. The tubing on the roof filtered the smoke before it emerged from the chimney. No fleet number can be seen on the trailer car, one of the fleet of eight built by the Starbuck Car & Wagon Co. Ltd of Birkenhead. A journey on the top deck could be a bleak affair! C. HALE's advert is on what was called a decency board or modesty panel, added to protect ladies' ankles from prying eyes and paid for by the profits that Mr Hale's 20 per cent off sale accrued! (Author's Collection)

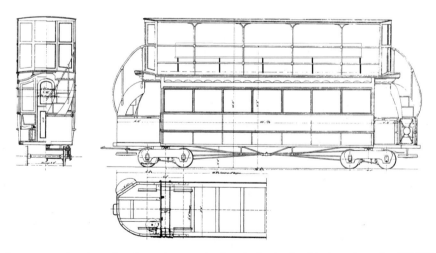

A cut-away drawing of a steam tramcar trailer similar to the kind used on the D&SST. (Author's Collection)

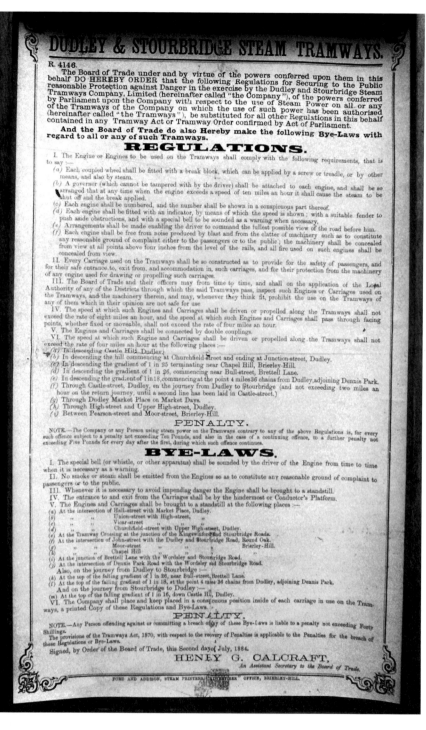

A copy of the D&SST's Regulations & Bye-Laws, which were carried and displayed in the lower saloon of each trailer car – they are dated 2 July 1884. *(Author's Collection)*

An unidentified combination of D&SST steam tramcar locomotive and trailer has just arrived at Dudley Station from Stourbridge – people can be seen standing on the top deck. The lamps, gate posts and fencing to the right were the entrance to the GWR side of Dudley Station – beyond this a noticeboard has 'GREAT WESTERN RAILWAY' on top of it. Dudley was in effect two stations – a GWR and a London & North Western Railway (L&NWR) one – sharing the same site but with different entrances, booking offices and platforms. *(Author's Collection)*

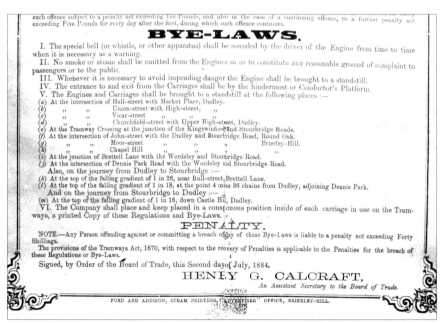

Time for a run to Stourbridge, but first a quick look at the bye-laws governing the operation of the D&SST's tramway. A total of thirteen Compulsory stops are listed – ten on the journey to Stourbridge and a further three on the run from there to Dudley. *(Author's Collection)*

A Stourbridge-bound D&SST steam tram works though Dudley Market Place with a wisp of smoke coming out of its locomotive's chimney. It has just passed THE GREAT TEA COMPANY and is now by a branch of PALETHORPE's. Based in nearby Tipton, the firm claimed to be the world's largest sausage producer, and their 'Royal Cambridge' variety won many awards. The horse and cart to the right was collecting parcels from the L&NWR's parcels office. *(Author's Collection)*

An engraving of Dudley Market Place from *Blocksidge's Illustrated Dudley Almanac* for 1887, depicting a D&SST steam tram on the final leg of a journey from Stourbridge. *(Peter Glews Collection)*

There are only a handful of photographs showing the D&SST's steam tramway in operation, and most of these, like this one, depict it in its final months. The location is Holly Hall, looking towards Dudley, with the tram in a passing loop. Behind the trap to the right, one of the traction poles for the electric tramway's overhead wires is already in place, dating this to the early months of 1899. *(Author's Collection)*

Probably the most detailed view of the D&SST's steam tramway in operation, taken in Brierley Hill High Street, with two trams in the passing loop in front of The Turk's Head Inn. There are more traction poles in place in the pavements on both sides and the track looks new. Add in the fact that the trees are coming into leaf and this would suggest a date of around May 1899 for the photograph. *(Author's Collection)*

A detail of the cars in the previous photograph shows the trailer car of the left-hand Dudley-bound to be No. 7. This affords splendid detail of both the locomotives and trailer cars used by the D&SST. *(Author's Collection)*

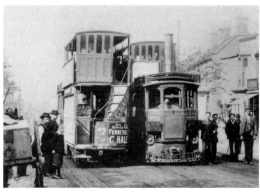

Black Country shop, and innkeepers have always been astute and quite a few of them sought to capitalise upon the tramway services that passed or stopped by their premises. For the keeper of THE TURK'S HEAD in Brierley Hill High Street the D&SST's steam tramway was a gift. There was a passing loop immediately outside his front door which was also the mid-point on the journey between Dudley and Stourbridge. As a result of this he had 'TRAM CAR WAITING ROOMS' painted atop his façade and doubtless welcomed many a tramway passenger fancying a break and a warm in front of the fire. There was stabling behind and the Shoeing Forge of W.H. Cheadle. *(Author's Collection)*

Shortly to become a refuge for tramway passengers was The Fish Inn at Amblecote, seen in the centre of this late nineteenth-century view of the junction between the Wordsley–Stourbridge and Wollaston roads which to this day is known by this inn's name. No traction poles are in sight so this is a view of the D&SST's steam tramway's lines as they approached Stourbridge. *(Author's Collection)*

Electrification

The history of Black Country tramways is almost exclusively one of private enterprise; its local authorities largely ignoring the option granted them in the 1870 Tramways Act to buy out tramway undertakings after twenty-one years. Thus when many of the local tramway companies' twenty-one years were up, mainly in the period from 1895 to 1900, they fell prey to larger tramway operators, notably the newly formed British Electric Traction Co. (BET), who bought the D&SST on 2 April 1898; the company's name being changed to the Dudley, Stourbridge & District Electric Traction Co. Ltd (DS&DET).

In addition to converting the Dudley–Stourbridge tramway to electric traction, powers were sought under The Dudley & District Light Railways Order, 1898 for the construction of seven additional lines:

- from a junction with the Dudley–Stourbridge tramway, along Kingswinford Road, Dudley, then leaving the Borough; passing through High Street, Pensnett, Dudley Road and High Street, Kingswinford, terminating at a point 50 yards beyond Market Street – 2 miles 7 furlongs 4.3 chains;
- from a junction with the above at Kingswinford Road/Market Street junction, along the latter, Portway (now Stream Road), High Street, Wordsley, to a junction with the Dudley–Stourbridge tramway at Brettell Lane, Amblecote – 2 miles 1.7 chains;
- a long connecting curve from the above to the tramway in Brettell Lane – 1.5 chains
- from the existing tramway terminus part way up Lower High Street, Stourbridge, passed the Town Clock at the junction with Market Street, through the very narrow High Street, to a terminus in Hagley Street, opposite the County Court – 3 furlongs 6.7 chains;
- from a junction with the main line in Queen's Cross, Dudley, down Blowers' Green Road, Cinder Bank, High Street, and Market Place, Netherton; then along Halesowen Road, to terminate at the boundary of Dudley Borough at the bridge over the Mousesweet Brook – 2 miles 8.4 chains;
- continuing from the end of the above along Halesowen Road to Old Hill Cross, Reddall Hill Road and (Upper) High Street, to Four Ways, Cradley Heath – 6 furlongs 9.8 chains, and;
- from the end of the above along High Street, Cradley Heath, terminating at the Five Ways – 2 furlongs 2.2 chains.

The above order was eventually granted on 1 November 1898.

The BET Co. placed a contract with Dick, Kerr & Co. for the relaying of the permanent way and the electrical equipment of the line from the Dudley boundary, near Hart's Hill, through Brierley Hill and Amblecote, to Stourbridge. A contract was placed with a local firm for the erection of a power station building and car shed, etc., at Hart's Hill, Brierley Hill. Early in May, 1898, a start was made on the reconstruction of the permanent way, and the first sod was turned for the foundations of the power station towards the end of that month.

Progress of the reconstruction is indicated by reports in the press:

- 12 December 1898 laying of electric tram rails in the Birmingham Road, on the side nearest the Castle;
- 29 January 1899 rails being laid in Birmingham Road, on the side nearest St Edmund's Schools;
- 17–22 April 1899 relaying of tracks in Dudley Market Place;
- 24–30 April 1899 laying of tracks in High Street;
- 5 May 1899 relaying outside St Thomas's Church;
- 22 May 1899 relaying the junction at Scott's Green for the Kingswinford route was commenced;
- 29 May 1899 relaying the junction at Queen's Cross for the Cradley Heath line.

Arrangements for the conversion, extension and provision of electrical power for the tramways were agreed with Dudley Corporation, although they were far from straightforward and even at this remove take some effort to comprehend. In essence, in terms of power, the lines within the Borough of Dudley were supplied with power by the Corporation from Springsmire, also the line to Cradley Heath. Power for the Kingswinford route, for 60 per cent of the Dudley–Stourbridge main line and for the Kinver and Lye routes was generated at the company's station at Brierley Hill, where were also the offices and main car sheds and repair shops. The Brierley Hill power station contained three horizontal Ball & Wood engines, connected direct to GE 6-pole 100kw generators.

DUDLEY
Corporation Electric Supply
Dudley Corporation Electrical Power Station

SIZE.—The total capacity of the dynamos is, at the present time, 1,600 kilowatts or 2,150 horse-power.
SUPPLY.—Current is supplied for lighting, power, heating, and traction purposes, at the following electrical pressures :—
    Lighting at 230 volts.   Heating at 230 volts.
    Power at 230 and 460 volts.   Trams at 500 volts.
TRAMWAYS.—The whole of the Trams in the Borough Boundary are supplied with current from the Springsmire Power Station.
LIGHTING.—Current is supplied on a large scale, both for public and private lighting.
POWER.—Current is also supplied for operating electric motors for almost all classes of trades in the Borough, there being connected to the cables, motors having a total brake horse-power of over 900.
HEATING.—A fair number of Electric Radiators, etc., are now being adopted, as this means of heating is cheap & scrupulously clean.

THE RATES OF CHARGES ARE AS FOLLOWS :—

LIGHTING.—Long Hour Consumers, over 1000 units
    per qr. ... ... 2¾d. per unit
    Including Private Houses, under 1000 units
    per qr. ... ... 3d. " "
    Theatres, Music Halls, Offices, Schools,
    and Works Lighting ... ... 3¼d. " "
    Short Hour Shops, over 1500 units per qr. 3d. " "
    Over 1000 units, and up to 1500 units per qr. 3¼d. " "
    Under 1000 ... ... 3½d. " "
POWER & HEATING.—Over 600 units per qr. ... 1d. " "
    From 300 to 600 units per qr. ... 1¼d. " "
    Under 300 ... ... 1½d. " "
Meter rents are charged to all consumers.
The Corporation's mains are laid free of charge into any premises within 20 yards of an existing cable, but are laid to greater distances at a reasonable guarantee for consumption of current.
OUTPUT.—At the close of the last Financial Year, the output of the Station was as follows :—

Units sold to Tramway Company ...	...	1,050,910
Units sold for Motors ...	...	413,727
Units sold for Lighting ...	...	422,333
Units sold for Public Street Lighting	...	135,237
Total ...	...	2,022,207

An advertisement placed by Dudley Corporation in 1909 promoting its electricity supply. The table at the bottom shows that 52 per cent of the total output of Springsmire Power Station was sold to the DS&DET. *(Author's Collection)*

The switchboard was also made by the General Electric Company of America. The condensing plant was situated in a chamber entirely below floor level and consisted of a Wheeler surface condenser and independent motor-driven and circulating pumps. Steam was supplied by three 30ft by 7ft 6in Lancashire boilers made by H & T Danks, water for these being stored in two cast-iron tanks holding 10,000 gallons each. Coal clack was delivered by barge direct to the boilers, and ashes were removed by the same means. To provide for more efficient supply of energy to districts remote from the power station, a battery of 240 Tudor cells was installed close to the junctions of the Kinver and Kingswinford lines with the main line. This battery had a capacity of 810 ampere hours and necessitated the installation of the third generating set at Brierley Hill.

The overhead was about equally divided between span-wire and bracket work. The rails were mostly 90lb and the rail bonds mostly of the 'Neptune' type. The cars were double-deck single truck powered by two GE 800hp 6-turn motors (later replaced by 4-turn motors for greater speed).

It is believed that during all this reconstruction the steam tram service was maintained as far as possible; cars no doubt operated to and from either side of the excavations, using both old and new tracks. This is evinced by the fact

The laying in of feeder cables for the new electric tramway's overhead wires in Dudley Market Place in 1899. Traction poles are in place and a trench has been dug for the feeder supply. This work was typically quite disruptive and brought many complaints from shopkeepers. In some places, such as Worcester, where the work overran, it became known as the tramway 'siege' or 'occupation'. (*Author's Collection*)

Photographs showing the reconstruction of Black Country tramways for electric operation are rare. This animated scene is from Sedgley and shows workers for George Law & Co. of Kidderminster using one of the BET's tower crane wagons to lower a traction pole in place. These were made from cast iron and extended almost half their height below ground, so lowering them into position was no easy task. This scene would have been repeated on numerous occasions in late 1898 and early 1899 as the Dudley–Stourbridge tramway was readied for electric operation. *(Author's Collection)*

that in June 1898 the Board of Trade granted the company a twelve-month extension of steam operation in view of the anticipated commencement of electric working in the autumn, and in June 1899, an extension of permission for steam working of one month, pending completion of electrical equipment, was also granted.

The power station at Hart's Hill was nearly completed, the track and overhead equipment was ready for use and the first batch of nine cars had been delivered, by about the middle of June 1899. Trial trips with the new tramcars were made around 18/19 June 1899, the Hart's Hill power plant being put to practical use for the first time. Further trials were carried out during the next few days and, early in July, for instruction of motormen, pending the Board of Trade inspection.

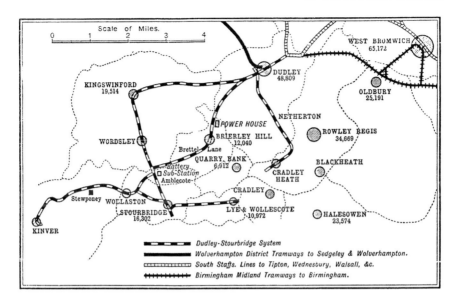

A map of the DS&DET's district and system, published in October 1902. The figures beneath some town names are their populations. *(Author's Collection)*

Things were not so advanced at Springsmire, and in order to have power available within time for the DS&DET to commence electric operation, Dudley Corporation equipped a temporary power station, which was ready for operation around 14 July 1899. This station was equipped with two Westinghouse compound engines and dynamos, each of 200hp, and was replaced by the new Springsmire Generating Station around February 1901.

The completed Dudley–Stourbridge electric tramway was inspected by the Board of Trade on 25 July and the line was opened throughout, from Dudley Station to Lower High Street, Stourbridge, the following day, 26 July 1899.

2

DUDLEY TO STOURBRIDGE

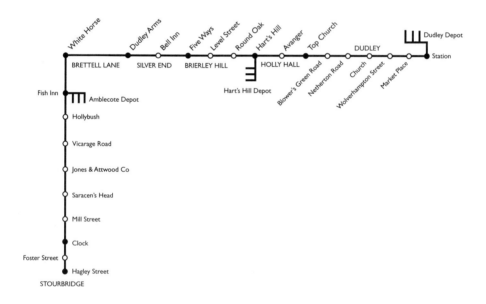

As noted above, the DS&DET opened its service from Dudley Station to Stourbridge on Wednesday, 26 July 1899 with a service of every five, ten or fifteen minutes until 22.45. The line was single track, with many passing loops. It started from Dudley Railway Station, where it made a junction with the Birmingham Midland and South Staffordshire systems. Only the main line cars run to this terminus; those from Cradley Heath and Kingswinford had their own terminus in Dudley Market Place. From here the line descended the whole way to Stourbridge. It ran past the principal depot and power station at Brierley Hill.

Let's take a trip on the newly opened line. The journey begins at the foot of Castle Hill, just east of the bridge carrying the road over the GWR lines. There is a basic cast-iron waiting shelter and a booking office, where through tickets to Kinver can be bought. The company's tracks connect here with those of Birmingham Corporation, reaching the city by two routes, via Oldbury or West Bromwich. Immediately beyond the rear of the car are facing point connections to the South Staffordshire tramways serving Tipton and Wednesbury.

Castle Hill is a 1-in-16 rising gradient. As the car moves off, the single line branches into a double track section, passing, on the right, the new Station Hotel (built in 1898), with a public drinking fountain at the junction of Trindle Road. On the left is Dudley Opera House, an imposing edifice opened in 1899 and a lodge to Dudley Castle. Otherwise the scene is green. Near the top of Castle Hill first the school (left), vicarage (right) and finally the Church of St Edmund are passed. After a nod towards a statue to William, Earl of Dudley, erected in 1888, the car swings left and the track becomes single along the narrow Castle Street, which is hemmed in on both sides by buildings. A passing loop begins at Fisher Street on the left and continues to Hall Street, where the Market Place opens up. The tracks again become double here, but are interlaced one within the other, such that, operationally, the section is single track. It runs to the left-hand side of the Market Place, which is defined by tall buildings on both sides and characterised by the noise and bustle of a busy market. Another passing loop begins at the end of the market, by the fountain donated by the Countess of Dudley, and extends to the junction with Stone Street on the right. From here it is a run up High Street, which also has imposing high buildings on both sides. Near the top, by Vicar Street on the right, there is a passing loop which extends almost to the junction with Old Mill Street on the right. Here a right-facing junction takes a single line to Stafford Street which connects with the tracks of the Wolverhampton & District Tramways in Snow Hill. To the left stands the Church of St Thomas, known by all as 'top church'; an imposing building with an iron core, erected in 1817.

From here the line begins to descend, passing Julia Hanson's brewery of around 1865 and a series of tightly packed housing courts on the right. A little past King Street, Blower's Green Road forks off left, with the lines to Netherton, Cradley Heath, Old Hill and Blackheath. Just past this point the main road becomes Queen's Cross and the tramway enters a lengthy double-track section. At first there is housing on both sides but this soon peters out on the left. The right-hand side of the road holds the most interest as, at Springs Mire, both the reservoir and pumping station of the South Staffordshire Waterworks Co. and the Dudley Corporation's Electricity Generating station are passed before the buildings of Hope Iron Works, opposite which the line becomes single again. This is a growing area called Scott's Green where the road name changes again to become Stourbridge Road. Here the line to Kingswinford via Pensnett branches off right. Almost immediately a mineral tramway line crosses the road and there is another passing loop. Waiting in this there are no houses to be seen but to the left is a brickworks and beyond the remains of Parkhead Colliery. After a scattering of houses on the right another passing loop is entered, opposite the Church of St Augustine to the left. On the right stands a small cluster of houses on a triangle of land stranded in the midst of a rather awkward junction with a road leading to Pensnett.

Just past the junctions with Hall and High streets (left) there is another public drinking fountain. This is Holly Hall. Down as far as Holly Street there are no buildings on the right, whereas the left-had side is a serried row of houses. Opposite Holly Street stands a fire station and Free Library. There are buildings on both sides now, mostly terraces to the left, until a school on the right. Here the buildings cease and the tramway enters another passing loop. This is Woodside. Glances right look over Fens Pool, a feeder reservoir to the canal and also where blast furnace slag was tipped from the Earl of Dudley's Round Oak Steelworks; to the left is Woodside Colliery. It is a short run to the next passing loop midway along which Hart's Hill is entered. There is dense housing, first on the left, where workers at Hartshill, Brierley Hill, Woodside and Round Oak iron and steel works live, and then also on the right, just as the loop ends. Just past Canal Street on the left is the tramway company's main depot, accessed by facing points in each direction off the single line. Built in 1899 this also accommodates an electricity generating station. Passing the depot there is another loop, which straddles both a canal and the lines of the Earl of Dudley's mineral railway, better known as the Pensnett Railway. Here on the right stands Hope Works, gas holder makers, and a glassworks left. A little further on the tramway crosses over the GWR's Stourbridge–Wolverhampton line and passes Round Oak station on the right. From here to the next passing loop attention is all to the left for this is the mighty Round Oak Iron & Steel Works the major employer in the area and a scene of perpetual activity, flame, smoke and sparks – all seen above and between buildings. The aforementioned passing loop is between John and Bent streets. Past it on the left is one of the Earl of Dudley's land sale coal wharfs.

The tramway now enters Brierley Hill. There is a passing loop just past the junction of Bank and Level streets which extends to Pearson Street on the left. Later doubled, the line along High Street Brierley Hill was originally single. The road is wide and densely built up on both sides. On the left stand the imposing Town Hall and the open market. A second passing loop begins just past Hall Street on the right; this leads to the works of Marsh & Baxter, manufacturers of pork products and Brierley Hill's second largest employer. The loop commences opposite the Red Lion Inn (right) and ends almost opposite the Roman Catholic Church of St Mary (left). This has been a fairly level part of the route but now it begins to descend more rapidly. The Church of St Michael dominates on a promontory to the right and there are houses to the left before another passing loop which ends by the opposing junctions of North and South streets. There are few houses beyond here until the next passing loop at Sliver End, just landscapes produced by collieries, some of which are still working. The end of the loop part straddles the junction with Lower Delph and beyond the line passes the settlement of Silver End on the right.

Here the road becomes Brettell Lane, which is also the name of the area. It is a vast accumulation of fireclay mines and brick works, all based around the extraction and working of beds of fireclay which has the highest silica content of any in the country. It is this that in the sixteenth century ended the relentless progress of itinerant Lorrainer glass makers up the land and gave birth to the local 'Stourbridge' glass industry. Somewhere here there are always brick kilns ablaze and at night these form quite a spectacle, visible both when passing through and when paused in two loops, the first being by the GWR's Brettell Lane Station and the second opposite Brettell Lane House, just before the junction with Collis Street. From here the line runs straight down Brettell Lane, to its junction with Stourbridge Road, Amblecote. The road has mostly housing along its left-hand side from Collis Street, but the right-hand side is devoid of anything before Oakfield House, where there is the first of two passing loops. Thereafter rows of terraced cottages predominate down to and including the second passing loop opposite Park Street on the left.

At the foot of Brettell Lane the tramway swings left. Here the line from Stourbridge to Kingswinford branches off right. The line runs down Stourbridge Road. At first this was single track but it was later doubled. Before this there was a passing loop opposite the end of Collis Street. At the far end of this loop the Kinver Light Railway branches off towards Wollaston. Buildings are again sparse; the glassworks of Webb, Corbett being the most noticeable (right). This character changes at the next passing loop, which is by the Holly Bush Inn (right) and a lodge to Corbett Hospital, formerly Hill House. Now there are houses on the left and a glassworks on the right. To the left the line passes the Church of Holy Trinity, Amblecote before entering a final passing loop, with the Stourbridge UDC Gas Works on the left and the works of Jones & Attwood on the right. Continuing on a short distance the tramway passes over the Stourbridge Canal and terminates just past the offices of the GWR's Stourbridge Town Goods Station by Mill Street.

There were many service variations over the years and some changes to the track and other infrastructure. The first of these concerned Dudley Market Place. In the spring of 1901 an idea emerged to create a tram terminus for the whole district there. This would involve a second track being laid through the market, but the scheme met with objections from market stall holders, residents and Councillors due to the loss of market tolls. A compromise was eventually reached and approved by Dudley Council on 1 October 1901. It provided for a long loop in the steep part of High Street and double track running from the Plume of Feathers Inn, in (Upper) High Street, to just beyond a new double track junction for the Cradley line in Queen's Cross. It connected with the existing double track on the main line and the loop at the top of Bath Hill. In addition, the plan called for two terminal sidings at the west end of the Market Place, adjacent to an existing loop. The new loop was completed by about the end of October 1901 and the Queen's Cross doubling by the end of November 1901. The service alterations came into force at once, Stourbridge line cars still running through to Dudley Station, whilst Cradley and Kingswinford line trams ran through to the Market Place, the former terminating on the siding nearest to the main line, whilst Kingswinford cars used the further siding.

Down the line there were several places in which on the single track sections sighting from passing loop to passing loop was difficult or impossible, causing delays to the service. A remedy was needed at two points in particular: in the High Streets at Brierley Hill and Amblecote. In the former it was agreed that several of the passing loops should be lengthened to give better sighting between them, and that the section from Five Ways through the High Street as far as the Post Office should be doubled, and to continue the doubling through

The foot of Castle Hill, Dudley, with one of the original single-decked cars, which were numbered 1-9. This may even be a photograph taken on or close to the opening of the Dudley–Stourbridge line on 26 July 1899. The lines the car is standing on are carried on a bridge over the railway lines into Dudley Station. Behind the tramcar is The Station Hotel, which opened on 28 May 1898. *(Author's Collection)*

Looking from the side of Castle Hill the tram in the previous view was standing on; this scene was photographed later in 1899. Car No. 15 was identical to Nos 1-9 but not delivered until September 1899; they took 28 passengers seated. Behind the sister car to the rear of No. 15 stands Dudley Opera House, which had only opened on 4 September 1899. The traction poles are particularly ornate. *(Author's Collection)*

the remainder of the main part of the street, to a point outside the Parish Church gates, at the top of the long hill through Brettell Lane to Amblecote. The track doubling in Brierley Hill High Street was completed from the Church gates to the Post Office by June 1903. The remaining section, to Five Ways, was not commenced until a month or so after this date, being completed by about October 1903. At Amblecote, the DS&DET proposed doubling the track on the main line from the White Horse Hotel, just short of Brettell Lane junction to a point immediately before Coalbournbrook junction. This double track section was laid in about November or December 1903.

At the foot of Castle Hill, the D&SDET lines met those of Birmingham Corporation (foreground right) and the South Staffordshire lines down Tipton Road. The shelter to the right of car No. 60 was the starting point for the Dudley–Stourbridge service. In the distance, below Castle Hill, Dudley a side view of Opera House can be seen. *(Author's Collection)*

A detail from the above image shows the shelter, to the right of car No. 60, which was the starting point for the Dudley – Stourbridge service. In the distance, below Castle Hill, a side view of Dudley Opera House can be seen. *(Author's Collection)*

'Entering Dudley' is the caption to this postcard view of the foot of Castle Hill which, then as now, was a main 'gateway' to the town. A better view is afforded of the façade of The Station Hotel and its public drinking fountain. Far right is the entrance to the GWR's side of Dudley Station, seen earlier with a steam tram. Here the tram is South Staffordshire Tramways Car No. 39, which was fitted with a top cover around 1910 to comply with an agreement with Walsall Corporation regarding the working of joint through services. A large tramcar, it seated 64 passengers. *(Author's Collection)*

The DS&DET's line connected with those of Birmingham Corporation at the foot of Castle Hill, where Car No.23, delivered in 1906, stands showing HANDSWORTH. These cars were fitted with top covers from 1911 onwards, giving clues as to the date of the photograph. *(Author's Collection)*

An engraving of Dudley Opera House, which its management used in advertisements. A tramcar has thoughtfully been included, but some traction poles have been omitted – leaving the overhead wires to support themselves! *(Author's Collection)*

The best-known view of the tram depot at the foot of Castle Hill, Dudley, is in the background of this photograph taken from the platform of the railway station. A staggered series of wooden buildings, there were two lines – or roads – inside and a third one outside, seen here with two cars on it. GWR 645 Class 0-6-0 saddle tank locomotive No.1513 was built in 1878 and is coupled to a wagon from Grazebrook's Collieries. *(Author's Collection)*

TIME TABLE.
DUDLEY, STOURBRIDGE & DISTRICT.

WEEK DAYS.

Cars leave Dudley for Stourbridge at 5 15, 5-40 a.m., and every 20 minutes until 7-30 a.m., then every 15 minutes until 1-0 p.m.; and also between 8-30 p m and 10-45 p.m., between 1-0 p.m. and 8-30 p.m. every 10 minutes. Leave Stourbridge for Dudley :--5-25 a.m , 6-0, 6-25, 6·55, 7·10, 7 30, 7-55, 8-15 a m. and every 15 minutes until 1-15 p.m., and also between 8-45 p.m. and 10 45 p.m. ; between 1-15 p m. and 8-45 p.m. every 10 minutes.
NOTE.—On Mondays and Saturdays extra cars will be run after 1-0 p.m.

SUNDAYS.

Dudley to Stourbridge, 10-0 a.m., 10-30, 11-0, 11-30, and every 15 minutes until 5-30 p.m., then every 10 minutes until 10-20 p.m. Stourbridge to Dudley, 10-15 a.m., 10-45, 11-15, 11-45, 12-15 p m., and every 15 minutes until 5-45 p.m., then every 10 minutes until 10-25 p.m. A frequent Service of Cars runs between **Dudley and Cradley, Dudley and Kingswinford, and Lye and Stourbridge,** meeting the Main Line Cars to Stourbridge.

KINVER LIGHT RAILWAY.

On this Route on week days cars commence running at 5-30 a.m. Kinver to Fish Inn, and 6-0 a.m. Fish Inn to Kinver, and will be increased or decreased according to the state of the weather and traffic. Last Car Kinver to Fish Inn 10-30 p.m. and Fish Inn to Kinver 11-0 p.m.

The same remarks apply to Sunday Services, commencing from Kinver at 9-0 a.m. and from Fish Inn at 9-30 a.m   Last Car Kinver to Fish Inn 10-0 p.m., Fish Inn to Kinver 10-30 p.m.

Time for a journey to Stourbridge by electric car. First, the timetable to peruse… *(Author's Collection)*

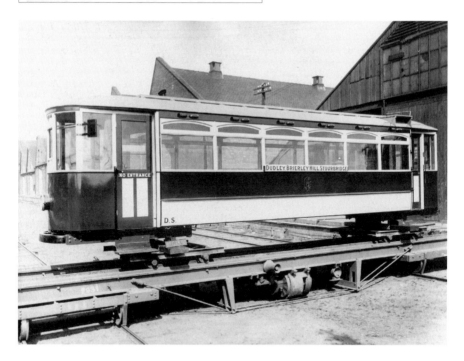

From 1913 onwards a standard design of single-deck tramcar was developed for use on the Black Country tramways. These were produced in large numbers from late 1919 onwards. The majority were built at the tramcar repairs works at Tividale, but a batch of ten bodies were built by the Brush Electrical Engineering Co. at Loughborough, where one of them was photographed on the works' traverser. The cars were numbered 71-80. *(Author's Collection)*

Loading at the Dudley Station shelter in 1929 was Car No. 29 of the standard design type. The cars seated 32. The sign on the traction pole reminds passengers that 'CARS LOAD HERE FOR BRIERLEY HILL STOURBRIDGE AND KINVER.' *(Peter Glews Collection)*

Below and to the left of Car No. 29 was Dudley Station. It was in fact two stations on one site. Here, to the left is the GWR station which was linked via the covered footbridge (centre) to the L&NWR (later LMS) station, which can be seen beneath the footbridge. The pannier tank locomotive in the bay platform to the left would have been working the line to Old Hill. *(Author's Collection)*

Standard Car No. 103 waiting at Dudley Station on Whit Monday (25 May) 1929. It was one of the last batches of these cars to be built – numbered 101-110 – and was built at Tividale in 1920. They feature all the innovations introduced on these cars, from new, including cushioned seats and a light to illuminate the destination board. No. 103 was one of a number of the cars whose windows had been modified to hinge outwards – as here – to make them more suitable for use on the KLR. *(Author's Collection)*

On 29 November 1920, Car No. 77 skidded on greasy rails and ran out of control down Castle Hill at about 40mph! The driver applied the new slipper brake and the car jumped the rails and collided with a lorry full of bones – which made the first on the scene fear that the accident had been worse than it was! It stopped when it went on to the pavement ran into Station Bridge, with about a third of it hanging over the 60ft drop to the rails below. The event was recorded by Victor Sims from Tipton who was the conductor on another tram that was passing at the time. Behind is probably the best view of the front of the DS&DET's depot at the foot of Castle Hill. *(Author's Collection)*

The journey to Stourbridge began with an ascent of Castle Hill, which has a ruling gradient of 1-in-16. After the entrance to the GWR railway station the main building of interest was Dudley Opera House, seen here. Next to this was a small 500-seater cinema called the Colosseum, opened by the Opera House's owner John Maurice Clement on 24 December 1910, but which closed when Clement died on 25 February 1912, dating this photograph to sometime in 1911. *(Author's Collection)*

A photograph from an article by Chalmers Roberts published in the American magazine *The World's Work* in 1903, in which he described 'A Trip on a Tram'. Probably taken in 1903, its original caption was: 'Tramways at the Dudley Castle Gates.' A 'Cradley bogie' car in the No. 52-59 series is working down Castle Hill with its rear indicator showing 'LYE'. *(Author's Collection)*

The Dudley–Stourbridge line along Castle Street can be seen in this commercial postcard view. Originally both the 'to' and 'from' Dudley lines were laid on the same side of the Market Place but, owing to restricted width, they were laid one within the other, or 'interlaced'. There were also separated overhead wires for

each line. To the left is the scale house for the public weighbridge, also left. As part of the reconstruction of the tramways through the Market Place, this weighbridge was moved to Stone Street in 1904. *(Author's Collection)*

The first of a series of three photographs of Dudley Market Place taken from an elevated position, which shows the track and weighbridge arrangements referred to in the previous photograph at a better advantage. *(Author's Collection)*

Both the market and the weighbridge are in full use in this second elevated view of Dudley Market Place. *(Author's Collection)*

In the last of the series of three photographs, an unusual moment has been captured. The market stalls have been stacked away and can be seen to the left of the cast-iron urinal. Finally there is also a tram, about to enter the interlaced section of track. *(Author's Collection)*

Another photograph from Chalmers Roberts' article, published in the American magazine *The World's Work* in 1903, in which he described 'A Trip on a Tram'. Probably taken in 1903, its original caption was: 'Types of cars in Dudley market-place.' At least two are identifiable: a 'Cradley bogie' car at right showing 'STOURBRIDGE' in its destination box and double-decker No. 39, waiting on one of the sidings, which was used on the Kingswinford line until it was transferred to the Wolverhampton–Dudley service in 1904. *(Author's Collection)*

The southern end of Dudley Market Place on a bright summer's day, with the market in full swing and a Dudley–Stourbridge tram working towards the camera. It is Car No. 30, which entered service early in 1901, and is showing DUDLEY as it works through the busy market. Outside the Maypole Dairies store they are promoting their MAYPOLE 1/6d TEA on a huge cut-out of a teapot! The Maypole stores originated in Wolverhampton in 1887 and grew to have over 1,000 stores nationwide. They disappeared from high streets in 1964. *(Author's Collection)*

When this photograph was published in December 1900 it was captioned: 'A View of the Market Square, Dudley.' It shows Car No.12, which was delivered in September 1899, working through the Market Place en route to Stourbridge and also affords a good view of the original track arrangement there. *(Author's Collection)*

A final view of the tram terminus in Dudley Market Place, this time in the late 1920s. An Inspector blocks the car's number as he chats to a passenger. The car was bound for Cradley Heath. *(Author's Collection)*

The junction of Wolverhampton Street (left) and Union Street (right) with High Street Dudley and a policeman on traffic duty. The Old Bush Hotel wrapped itself around the corner of Union Street. It was once owned by wine and spirit merchant James Cartwright, but was demolished in the early 1930s and replaced by a bank which is now a branch of Barclays. There were three cars in the Market Place terminus or working their way through it on this occasion, including two double-deckers and a standard single-decker. *(Author's Collection)*

A photograph of (Upper) High Street, Dudley, showing the single tramline and passing loop very clearly. Lipton stores began in Glasgow in 1871 and in 1888 began to sell their own tea. They merged with Home & Colonial stores in 1929 and traded under that name thereafter. There is a compulsory 'CARS STOP HERE' sign on the traction pole on the left. *(Author's Collection)*

A view of (Upper) High Street Dudley from the late 1920s with a standard single-decked car in the passing loop. J. Bunce was a drapers' store and Bunney's was a china shop. Despite the year, the visible transport is only horse or people-powered! *(Author's Collection)*

A detail from an earlier photograph showing the passing loop in (Upper) High Street, Dudley. The track is rather 'undulating' and there is a complete absence of traffic apart from a heavily laden handcart, which has attracted the attention of a dachshund. *(Author's Collection)*

(Upper) High Street, Dudley, decorated for the Coronation of King Edward VII on 9 August 1903. There are at least four newspaper sellers to view, probably selling Coronation Special Editions. Many of the buildings on the left here survive, but most of those on the right were swept away for the Trident Centre in the early 1970s. This point was a section feeder, a point where power was fed into the system – note the cable wrapped around the side arm. The decorative horns were used to carry telegraph wires. *(Author's Collection)*

There are gaps in the photographs showing the Dudley–Stourbridge line, such as in between Queen's Cross and down Stourbridge Road. Coverage resumes here with the first in a series of five photographs taken to record water main laying works at Scott's Green, Dudley – this one on 13 November 1922. The tramway somehow worked its way along the earth embankment! *(Author's Collection)*

This second view is from more or less the same vantage point but was taken on 23 February 1923, when the water main was actually in place. As workers continue their tasks, two DS&DET staff stand by as a double-decker car works through en route to Stourbridge. There are no passengers to be seen, so possibly this records a clearance test on some realigned trackwork. *(Author's Collection)*

Another photograph taken on 23 February 1923 of the water main works at Scott's Green shows that the tramlines were laid on sleepers like railway track. A tramway official can be seen as well as a man in a trilby hat, possibly the engineers in charge of the works. A Stourbridge-bound car approaches! *(Author's Collection)*

The Church of St Augustine of Hippo was erected at Holly Hall in 1889. This postcard view shows it with a Stourbridge tram passing along Stourbridge Road. As cars approached the stop seen outside the church, Conductor's used to call out 'Avanger'. The lack of overhead wires is explained by the fact that this is a coloured postcard – they were painted out in the colouring! *(Author's Collection)*

The DS&DET's main car depot had been built adjacent to the Hart's Hill Generating Station and was capable of storing twenty-four cars, on eight tracks served by turntables. There was also a small repair section. Seen here in its later days after closure as a West Midlands Travel bus garage, the tram depot was the brick building side-on in this view. The buildings were demolished in November 2011. *(Author)*

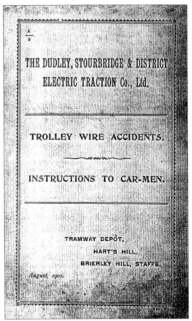

The BET Monthly Gazette for October 1903 contained the following description of the power station at Hart's Hill, which: 'contained three horizontal Ball & Wood engines, connected direct to GE 6-pole 100kw generators. The switchboard was also made by the GE Company of America. Condensing plant was situated in a chamber entirely below floor level and consisted of a Wheeler surface condenser and independent motor-driven and circulating pumps. Steam was supplied by three 30ft by 7ft 6in Lancashire boilers made by H & T Danks, water for these being stored in two cast-iron tanks holding 10,000 gallons each. Coal clack was delivered by barge direct to the boilers, and ashes were removed by the same means.' *(Author's Collection)*

Tram crew – or 'Car-Men' – were issued with various sets of instructions, some of which related to specific lines; others to specific situations or problems – such as Trolley Wire Accidents as here. *(Author's Collection)*

Every Car must carry two keys for feeder pillars, a pair of rubber gloves in good repair, and a pair of cutting pliers with insulated handles. All Carmen must know how to switch off current at the feeder pillars, and how to telephone to the works. On hearing of an accident get a car as near the spot as possible, assist the police to get the current cut off at feeder pillars, and if no one is entangled leave fallen wires alone until current is switched off, then cut hanging wires to clear street for traffic. Usually this can be done easily from the roof of a car.

Telephone, or send message by quickest means available to the works, giving particulars of the trouble, and saying how near Cars can be run on either side to facilitate the repairs.

The Source of Danger.—Trolley wires being electrically charged to a rather high pressure will give a severe shock to any person or animal by simple contact with the skin, or wet clothing. Unless the contact be prolonged, as by entanglement with a wire resting on the trolley wire, such a shock is not likely to cause serious damage to a healthy person. Horses, however, are very susceptible, and may be killed by a contact of short duration.

Keep Away.—Should a trolley wire, or other wire falling across it come down from any cause, the first action should be to keep all persons and vehicles at a safe distance.

To Cut Off Current.—At every half mile along the tramway are "feeder pillars" containing switches by which the current may be cut off from the trolley wires. Generally each half mile length of trolley wire is connected at both ends through the feeder pillars to underground cables, so the switches must be turned off at each end of the section. Every Car carries two keys of the pillars,

and two are kept at all neighbouring Police Stations. Therefore someone should go along the tramway in each direction until he finds a feeder pillar, hailing the first car he sees or meets, and ask the driver to turn the current off from the section, or the keys can be obtained from the nearest Police Station, and current turned off by the Police Officers. Messages should be telephoned or sent by the quickest means available, to the Tramway Power House or Office. Unless some person or animal is entangled the wires should not be touched by anyone except the Tramway Officers until it is ascertained that the current has been cut off.

To Release Entangled Persons.—Should anyone have become entangled in a fallen wire the readiest method of release, calling for no special tools, is to press some part of the wire between the entangled person and the trolley wire firmly upon the tramway rail with some wooden implement. This will certainly make the wire beyond the rail "dead," and the person should be disentangled whilst the wire is being held steadily to the rail. Small telephone wires will usually be fused by being put in contact with the rail.

The above process will be quicker than waiting for insulated pliers and rubber gloves, unless a tramcar should happen to be close to the spot.

"Live" wires can be cut with entire safety with ordinary pliers or nippers if the operator be mounted on a pair of steps, or on a car or van, standing on the wooden portion only. Any person injured should have immediate medical attention. If unconscious, he should be treated exactly as if apparently drowned, by artificial respiration, which must be commenced without the least delay.

By Order.

The contents of the above instructions. They make grim reading in places. 'Horses … may be killed by a contact of short duration', and procedures 'To Release Entangled Persons.' *(Author's Collection)*

Writing in the American magazine *The World's Work* in 1903, Chalmers Roberts described 'A Trip on a Tram': 'Later we reach picturesque Dudley … This is the least attractive portion of the journey, for it lies through the heart of the Black Country, and one feels on every hand the heavy stress of the working world. You look out everywhere on a cloud of smoke that seems to cover the earth and to dim a horizon serrated with chimneystacks. On you go over bridges which cover murky

canals, through motley suburbs, past great iron mills overpowering, terrible, sometimes even artistic in the forest of unbeautiful chimneys about them, for ever vomiting gaseous volumes to take on every shade and hue of the changing light'. The above image from his article was captioned 'In the heart of the Black Country'. *(Author's Collection)*

Car No. 18 posed on the Dudley–Stourbridge line with Motorman, Conductor and a passenger, who is possibly a DS&DET Company official. The precise location of this view, taken on a very foggy day, is unknown. *(Author's Collection)*

When Inclosure Commissioners surveyed Brierley Hill in the 1780s, with great forethought they allowed a width of 60ft for the High Street. This allowed doubling of the tramlines in June 1903 and provided a road along which trams and other vehicles did not interfere with each other. Brierley Hill's market can be seen at left in the days before it was itself 'enclosed'. *(Author's Collection)*

Workers and officials of the British Insulated Callender Cable Co. pose either side of work to lay in the electricity supply to the shops and houses in Brierley Hill High Street as a Stourbridge-bound car passes the market. The Barber's next to the Butter Stores (left) was a collecting office for the Tramways Parcels service which commenced early in 1906. *(Janet Bayard-Jones)*

A cortège formed of horse-drawn vehicles from Cartwright's undertakers photographed at Five Ways in Brierley Hill High Street, at the corner with Cottage and Mill streets. There is a hearse and four other vehicles. The Town Arms has an elegant frontage and the taller building behind was a shop for Marsh & Baxter, a local bacon curer and maker of pork products. *(Author's Collection)*

A detail from the previous image shows that Cartwright's cortege was in fact holding up two Stourbridge-bound cars. In the foreground a boy waits on the back of a milk cart which has been surrounded by sheep. These were bound for the animal market in Albion Street. Behind is a water cart which was used to spray the roads to keep down dust. *(Author's Collection)*

In the early months of 1918, six Mark IV male tanks toured the towns and cities of England, Scotland and Wales, the primary purpose of the campaign was to promote the sale of government War Bonds and War Savings Certificates. Here is tank No. 113, named *Julian* at the top of Church Street, Brierley Hill, with a vicar addressing a large crowd. A Stourbridge service car has been 'trapped' by the throng. The banner reads: 'PUT ALL YOUR SAVINGS IN THE BRIERLEY HILL TANK BANK.' *(Author's Collection)*

Julian's arrival in Brierley Hill was heralded by a procession lead by a military band. It was clearly a very wet spring day – note the umbrellas and the wet road. The tank is passing the junction of North and South streets with Church Hill. Another car has been delayed by proceedings. In the background the glow from various brick kilns can be seen. *(Author's Collection)*

The Dudley–Stourbridge line next passed along Brettell Lane, which was then a hive of firebrick works. One of the biggest firms was Harris & Pearson, which was founded in 1852. In 1903, the firm acquired a controlling interest in firebrick firm Trotter, Haines & Corbett. Here is their works' outing waiting to depart from the front of Harris & Pearson's offices on 4 July 1925, which are now restored and listed grade II. *(Author's Collection)*

There is then another gap in the photographs showing the Dudley–Stourbridge line until the lower end of Brettell Lane, and its junction with High Street, Amblecote. This view is from the early years of the tramway in the 1900s and shows a Stourbridge-bound double-decked car. Although the general aspect of Brettell Lane has not changed, very few of these buildings survive, save for a few cottages on the right. *(Author's Collection)*

A view looking up Brettell Lane from the corner with High Street, Amblecote. The car is in more or less the same place as the one in the previous image. *(Author's Collection)*

The Kingswinford–Stourbridge line is in the foreground in this commercial postcard view of the end of Brettell Lane. The White Horse Hotel (now The Maverick) survives as do many of the properties on the right. There is a compulsory stop sign on the traction pole outside the pub. This is another coloured postcard, so no overhead wires! *(Author's Collection)*

A close up of the junction between the Dudley–Stourbridge and Kingswinford–Stourbridge lines in Amblecote, with a group of people at the tram stop. *(History of Wollaston Group)*

High Street, Amblecote seen from outside the DS&DET's Amblecote depot, with Collis Street on the right and Wollaston Road on the left. The section of line doubled by December 1903 can be seen narrowing back to a single one and the connection to the KLR can be seen bottom left. The prominent bay window on the COFFEE & TEA ROOMS at right used to be a turnpike tollhouse. *(Author's Collection)*

The Fish Inn on the corner of High Street, Amblecote and Wollaston Road has given its name to this busy road junction, which is called 'The Fish'. Here a KLR car waits to load before departure. Behind is the Coalbournhill Glassworks. The firm of Webb Corbett, founded in 1897, had a disastrous fire at their original White House works on 31 March 1914 and moved to this site shortly afterwards. *(Author's Collection)*

A 'Cradley bogie' car – possibly No. 56 – in the yard at the DS&DET's Amblecote depot. It has been decorated to promote 'STOURBRIDGE SHOPPING WEEK', and has been fitted with coloured light bulbs around the windows and the trolley poles have been candy-striped! Two years fit the dates shown, but the most likely is 7-12 November 1910. *(Author's Collection)*

High Street, Amblecote, outside the main gates to the Corbett Hospital (extreme right). A double-decked car is working towards Stourbridge and is stopped by a passing loop. A plate marking fare stage 22 is on the traction pole on the right. All the poles have white paint on them, which was added during 1916 after the first Zeppelin raids over the Black Country prompted night-time blackouts. The Corbett Hospital began as The Hill, a house bought by local man made good, the salt king John Corbett, who refurbished it as a hospital and endowed it to the local people on 31 July 1893. *(Author's Collection)*

The original Stourbridge tram terminus was just past here by the junction with Mill Street. This photograph was taken after the tramway service has closed. The tall building on the left was the offices to Stourbridge Goods Station, which opened on 1 January 1880 and closed on 5 July 1965. Beyond the traction pole on the right can be seen the parapets to the bridge over the River Stour from which the town takes its name. *(Author's Collection)*

3

DUDLEY (STAFFORD STREET) TO DUDLEY (WOLVERHAMPTON STREET)

This short 2 furlongs 2.7 chains long line was promoted and built to connect the D&SDET's lines with those of the tramway company which operated the line between Dudley and Wolverhampton via Sedgley. It was contained in the Dudley & District Light Railways (Extensions) Order 1899, which received its powers on 3 April 1900. Built quickly, the line was inspected on 28 September 1900 – the same day as the Cradley Heath one.

The Dudley to Sedgley service was opened on 3 October 1900, on behalf of the BET Company, cars ran from a dead-end terminus near the Post Office, in Wolverhampton Street, Dudley; the Stafford Street connecting line was also brought into use, although no passenger service was, as yet, operated over it. This Sedgley section, together with the Stafford Street line, was transferred by the BET from 1 February 1901, to the newly formed Wolverhampton District Electric Tramways Limited (WDET), but the D&SDET continued to operate

This photograph shows the only known glimpse of the short Stafford Street line. The location is High Street, Dudley, just down from 'Top Church', looking across towards The Three Crowns Inn and a newsagents and tobacconists shop which stands on the corner with Stafford Street. One of the traction poles for the Stafford Street overhead wires can be seen on the right. (Author's Collection)

it for some considerable time. On 13 November 1902, the WDET cars from Bilston and Sedgley commenced to run via Stafford Street, Dudley, High Street and the Market Place to the station terminus. In later years, the Stafford Street connecting line saw less and less regular use and it closed in 1926.

WDET car No. 10 of 1901 approaching Dudley along Wolverhampton Street in the early years of operation of the line, probably to the dead-end terminus near the Post Office there, with a horse bus in the distance. *(Author's Collection)*

Seen working away from Wolverhampton Street, Dudley, towards Wolverhampton is WDET car No. 30, a 70-seater double-decker mounted on maximum traction bogies with their pony (smaller) wheel leading. Flags abound, so this was clearly a special occasion, such as the annual Dudley Pageant, Empire Day or possibly even the Coronation of King Edward VII. *(Author's Collection)*

4

DUDLEY TO CRADLEY HEATH VIA NETHERTON

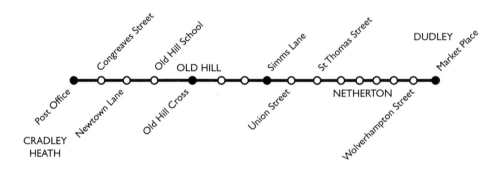

Construction on the Cradley Heath line was well advanced when the main Dudley–Stourbridge one opened. Indeed, by the second week of July 1899, the contractors had proceeded as far as Netherton. Construction seems to have been practically completed by January 1900, although it appears to have taken a very long time to finish the overhead and electrical equipment. The Cradley Heath line was finally completed early in July 1900, but still did not open, causing the Dudley Herald to comment on 22 September 1900 that: 'the Cradley Heath… lines had all been completed for some weeks, and that rumour had it that grass is growing on the tracks and that there is no likelihood yet of trams running…!' The delay was but short as public traffic on the Cradley Heath line commenced on Monday, 1 October 1900.

On the Cradley line, owing to several stiff hills, the local authorities would only permit single-decked cars. The line branches off the main Dudley–Stourbridge one at Queen's Cross, descending rapidly down Blower's Green Road. The land is largely undeveloped. On the right the public baths are passed and on the left the rear of the corporation cemetery. There are no buildings adjacent to the tramway before Blower's Green House on the left, just before the road passes over the main GWR line between Stourbridge and Dudley. Just beyond a mineral tramway crosses the road and the first passing loop on the line is entered. Still descending, the line encounters buildings on the left, first a Messiah Baptist Chapel, then a row of terraced cottages – this is Cinder Bank. Netherton New Road branches off on the left, doubling back on the main road, and here is the next passing loop. This is opposite Jubilee Terrace, a regimented row of regular terraced cottages. Simms Lane forks off right and immediately there are buildings on both sides; right a malthouse complex and school, left more houses and an inn. Another passing loop bestrides the junction with St Thomas's Street. Now most of the buildings are on the right. Down to the junction with Northfield Road on the left, where there is another passing loop, the southern tip of which aligns with Netherton Market Place.

A left-hand bend and still descending, the line enters Halesowen Road. As Cradley Road forks off right there is another passing loop starting opposite the Junction Inn. Now Halesowen Road is densely developed on both sides. Between Chapel and Washington streets, both on the right, there is another passing loop. Beyond this, left is the GWR's Withymoor Goods Station and

Each of the DS&DET's lines had its own set of 'REGULATIONS AND INSTRUCTIONS TO MOTORMEN'; this is the cover of the version for the 'CRADLEY HEATH ROUTE' which was issued in October 1900. (Author's Collection)

Each 'REGULATIONS AND INSTRUCTIONS' book contained details of speed restrictions and compulsory stops, such as these for the Dudley–Cradley Heath route. Of particular note here is IV (e) which records that private mineral railways crossed the road and the tramway in two places. (Author's Collection)

canal transhipment basin; to the right is Noah Hingley & Sons Netherton Works, where, in 1911, the anchors and chain for the ill-fated RMS *Titanic* would be made – this is Primrosehill. Past the crossroad junction with Saltwells Road there is another passing loop opposite cottages on the left and a school on the right. The descent continues through collieries on both sides to another passing loop before a dip where the Mousesweet Brook passes beneath the road. Yet another passing loop next, whose southern end aligns with the junction with Cox's Lane on the left. The line turns right into Reddall Hill Road, the curve also being a passing loop. Past this point the road is heavily developed on both sides and more passing loops, first opposite Reddall Hill Schools and then opposite Newtown Street on the right. This is Spinner's End.

Past the Church of St Luke and, first, its vicarage; then over Four Ways into High Street, where there is another passing loop opposite The Holly Bush Inn, which has the timber Empire Theatre behind it. Down High Street to Five Ways, where the line turns left into Cradley Road, where there is the last passing loop and, just beyond it, the end of the line.

Public praise for the trams was immediate and lavish, but, without any warning, from the following Thursday morning, 4 October 1900, the cars ceased to operate. No explanation was given to the public, but it appears that the line had been opened in error, the official Board of Trade Certificate having not been received. The line was idle for more than a fortnight, during which time rumours spread that the hold-up in granting the Certificate was due to a lack of brake power on the cars on the steep gradients on the new route, especially that of Bath Hill, Dudley, immediately after leaving the main line. This was in fact correct; the Board of Trade had specified that the cars must be fitted with slipper brakes to ensure safety on the gradients. Their Certificate was eventually received and the line re-opened on 19 October 1900, the service operating from Dudley Station to Five Ways, Cradley Heath every twelve, fifteen or twenty minutes until 23.00.

Three of the D&SDET's routes were worked by very distinctive types of cars: the Cradley Heath, Kingswinford and Kinver lines. Gradients on the Cradley Heath line precluded the use of double-deck cars so new, long single-deck cars were built for it. These came into service about October or November 1902 releasing other single-deckers for other services. They were always known as the 'Cradley' or 'Cradley bogie' car, although they were later operated on other services, notably the KLR. Built by Brush, these closed combination single-deckers had equal-wheel bogies and four-motor drive. The bodies had a centre compartment and two end sections, seating 52 passengers; there were eight cars in all, numbered 52-59.

All the adverse factors referred to above under the Dudley–Stourbridge main line also worked against the Cradley Heath line, yet, despite its gradients and occasional subsidence en route, it remained open right up to the end of the 1920s, closing on Tuesday, 31 December 1929.

High Street, Netherton in the early years of the opening of the Dudley–Cradley Heath line. A car is descending through Market Place and is about to pass along Halesowen Road, to the right. The traction poles, complete with their support brackets and scrollwork, are very impressive. Unfortunately, being a coloured postcard, the wires themselves have been painted out! *(Author's Collection)*

A little further down Halesowen Road, Netherton in the 1920s. The white-painted pub behind the motor van is the same building as the one behind the girl standing on the left in the previous image. All of the ornamental scrollwork has been removed from the traction poles. Centre left is a public drinking fountain and behind that a public weighbridge and its machine house. *(Author's Collection)*

The hilly nature of the Dudley–Cradley Heath line precluded the use double-decked cars so the DS&DET ordered eight single-deckers with an equal seating capacity. To achieve this, the cars were very long – 44ft 8in – but seated 52. Car No. 59 here was the highest-numbered one and is seen in (Upper) High Street, Cradley Heath, when new. (*Author's Collection*)

The Dudley–Cradley Heath line passing through Four Ways, which marks the point where (Upper) High Street becomes High Street. The imposing building to the right was the United Counties Bank, later part of Barclays. (*Author's Collection*)

A very detailed and precise record survives of the top part of Cradley Heath High Street on a particular day – Monday, 3 October 1910; this was the second and last procession and public meeting in association with the Women Chainmakers' Strike, which was drawing to a successful conclusion. Here a crowd, mainly of women and children, wait for the procession to arrive from Cradley Heath & Cradley Station, with Four Ways and the Church of St Luke in the background. *(Author's Collection)*

This view of the crowds awaiting the arrival of the procession from Cradley Heath & Cradley Station on Monday, 3 October 1910 also affords a good view of this part of the Dudley–Cradley Heath line. *(Author's Collection)*

The procession arrives and is clearly holding up a service tram in the distance. *(Author's Collection)*

Towards the rear of the procession rode Mary McArthur (1880–1921), a trade unionist and women's rights campaigner, who co-ordinated the Women Chainmakers' Strike. *(Author's Collection)*

This detail from the previous photograph reveals that it was a Dudley-bound car delayed by the Strike procession. *(Author's Collection)*

Mary McArthur seen here arriving outside the Empire Theatre. Some boys have found one traction pole very useful as a vantage point! *(Author's Collection)*

The Strike Rally at The Empire Theatre on Monday, 3 October 1910 where the crowd was addressed by Mary McArthur and Arthur Henderson, MP. *(Author's Collection)*

Looking down High Street, Cradley Heath, along a very deserted road towards Five Ways. *(Author's Collection)*

Looking up High Street, Cradley Heath with a Dudley-bound car working away from the camera. The flags and decorations may have been part of the annual Empire Day celebrations, held each year on 24 May. *(Author's Collection)*

A more everyday scene in more or less the same location with, again, a Dudley-bound car. *(Author's Collection)*

Emergency repairs are being undertaken in High Street, Cradley Heath following a mining subsidence on 19 February 1914, when approximately 200 yards of the road collapsed and fell up to 3ft in places. Many of the properties were shored up with timber supports as they leaned precariously towards the street. At the centre of the newly appeared dip in the road, the Talbot Hotel to the left was particularly affected. Upon investigation the problem was identified as being in the workings of Messrs Parsons & Co.'s Stour Colliery, which was located in an area called 'Rattlechain' off Graingers Lane – a short distance from the Corngreaves Hotel. A reopened mine; the miners had removed coal from supporting pillars! (*Author's Collection*)

The end of Cradley Heath High Street from Cradley Road, showing the curve leading to the terminus. On the corner of the High Street stands The Five Ways Inn. (*Black Country History in Photographs*)

The terminus of the Cradley Heath line in Cradley Road, where a car has just arrived and passengers are leaving by the rear platform. (*Black Country History in Photographs*)

The funeral cortége for Motorman Martin Cadman, who died on 5 February 1901 after struggling to get his car back to Hart's Hill depot in the teeth of a fierce snow storm the previous evening. It is pictured in Stourbridge Road, close to Hart's Hill. Note the crowds behind and to the side of the trams! *(Author's Collection)*

There was an early tragedy associated with the line. On 4 February 1901, a heavy snowstorm caused some disruption to the system. Motorman Martin Cadman, who worked on the Cradley line, had a tremendous struggle to get his open fronted car back to Hart's Hill depot in the teeth of the snow storm that night. He suffered from heart disease and, after walking home in the small hours, died suddenly, his exertions having been too much for him. In honour of his devotion he was given a tramway funeral from his home to the nearest point on the line to St James's Church, Wollaston, where he was buried. As the *County Express* reported:

> The arrangements were made at Hart's Hill Depot by the Manager, Mr Smith, and Fitter Mr Gardner. A wagon was made out of part of one of the old steam cars and fitted up for carrying the coffin and wreaths, which stood on a platform some 18 inches high above the wheels, and was draped with black and purple. A canopy over the top was similarly draped, and employees of the company in uniform with black bands on the arm, formed a guard around the remains. In front was a car, also draped, conveying the bearers, and other company employees, some 32 in all. At the rear was a third car, likewise with mourning insignia, carrying the widow and mourners. When the procession started from Martin's late home at Queen's Cross there was quite a crowd of 2,000 present. It had been decided to bury the deceased at Wollaston, and the sight of so unique a spectacle was witnessed by many thousands of people, in fact the road from Dudley to Wollaston was practically lined all the way. At Coalbournbrook the procession had to be reversed, and proceeded to the junction of the roads near to Wollaston Church, from whence the body was carried by bearers to the Church.

It is likely that this is one of the very first uses of the KLR, some two months before it opened.

5

DUDLEY TO
KINGSWINFORD VIA PENSNETT

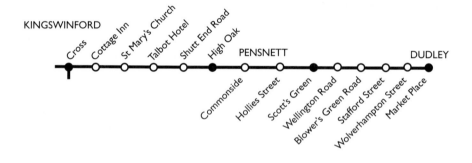

As with the Cradley Heath line, construction on the Kingswinford via Pensnett line had commenced when the Dudley–Stourbridge main line opened in July 1899. By the second week of that month, contractors had proceeded as far as Pensnett from Holly Hall, on the Kingswinford route. The permanent way of the Kingswinford line had been practically completed by January 1900 – but it did not open. By the middle of September 1900, the local press stated that trial trips had been made over the line, but why this line was not ready for inspection at the same time as the other lines is not clear. The BET's *Monthly Gazette* for October 1900 stated that the Board of Trade had been notified that the line was ready for inspection. This was carried out on 9 November 1900, but it was only officially opened, after further local complaints about the delay, on 6 December 1900, public traffic commencing on the following day.

The Kingswinford line branches off right from the main line at Scott's Green. For its first section the route is devoid of buildings on either side, although to the right it paralleled a mineral railway embankment. There are three passing loops, each end of and in the middle of this section. The third loop follows the curve that the line takes into High Street, Pensnett at Lowtown. Still devoid of buildings the tramway proceeds to its next passing loop, which is opposite Hollies Farm on the right. More and more buildings appear on the left whilst on the right is the drive to the Church of St Mark, where there is another passing loop.

In this part of High Street the left-hand side is fully developed whilst the right-hand one is mainly green. Almost immediately after the next passing loop the line passes over a branch of the Earl of Dudley's mineral railway serving, amongst others, Himley Colliery.

The tramway enters High Oak where there is a passing loop which ends by the eponymous pub and the junction with Commonside on the left. From this point the line begins to descend. Just past the junction with the as yet unnamed Tansey Green Road on the right there is one passing loop, with another one opposite the junction with the also yet to be named Dreadnought Road. Immediately after this the tramway crosses the GWR's Kingswinford Branch and, after passing a saw mill (left) and lime works (right), crosses the Stourbridge Extension Canal by means of Lench's Bridge, immediately entering a passing loop. The scene is again almost devoid of buildings. This is an area known locally as 'The Planet', an area of fireclay extraction and brick and tile making. The next passing loop is opposite Kingswinford Works, a brick and tile manufactory, on the left. The line now enters the outskirts of Kingswinford village, with the Church of St Mary on the right. On the approach to The Cross, there is a marked contrast on either side of the tram. There are buildings on the right but to the left the landscape is scarred by sand extraction. High Street bends right, where there is a passing loop, and the left-hand side houses a school and the old Bradley Hall of 1596. After a small gap in the buildings, The Cross is reached. Here the tramway curves right then left to enter Summerhill where, after a long passing loop, it terminates.

The service was initially operated in two sections. One from Dudley Station ran via the Market Place, Scott's Green junction and Pensnett, to a terminus on the stub-end track at Kingswinford. Here cars connected with the other service, running through Wordsley to a junction with the main line at Brettell Lane, Amblecote, and then to the Stourbridge terminus. The service was every fifteen, twenty or thirty minutes.

In common with many British tramways, the Black Country ones found that the operation of open-top, double-deck cars presented one major disadvantage. This was that, although very many passengers preferred the exhilarating open-air ride in good weather, very few wanted to travel outside in really wet or wintry conditions. Indeed, in rush hours during the winter, the upper decks were hardly used. In addition, smokers complained about being forced to use the saloon in bad weather, where no smoking was allowed. Permanently closed top covers had been tried on some tramway systems, without much success, because passengers preferred an open car in good weather. Removable and collapsible covers had not proven very satisfactory. C.R. Bellamy, the General Manager of Liverpool Corporation Tramways, designed a type of cover to attempt to solve this difficulty in 1902; the first experimental car fitted with one went into service in Liverpool in September 1902. It was so successful that, several hundred cars fitted with 'Bellamy' top covers of similar though somewhat improved design were in operation in the city within a year or two.

The D&SDET decided to try out this type of top cover for some of its open-top cars running on the Dudley–Stourbridge main line and the Kingswinford ones. Six cars of the No. 23-38 series were fitted with covers similar to the improved Liverpool designs. These were somewhat longer than the three-windowed saloon of the car, had five windows per side, which could be dropped to a completely open position; five corresponding sliding sections in each side of the roof could be opened by being slid under the solid centre portion, with the result that nearly two-thirds of the roof area could be opened. The short open balconies were completely uncovered. This improvement cost about £100 a car, equal to about 14 per cent of the vehicle's original cost. Nos 32, 33, 34, 35, 36 and 38 were fitted and they went into service in early April 1904 being limited to the Dudley–Stourbridge and Kingswinford lines. An immediate success, they earned an average of 2*d* per car mile more than open-top cars and, during August 1904, their receipts had been as high as 16*d* per car mile, in some cases.

Passengers bound for Kingswinford who needed to change cars at Scott's Green complained that they had to wait in the middle of the road in all weathers. Eventually the D&SDET responded in 1909 by erecting a new waiting room. This shelter looked very like the ones commonly seen on seaside promenades all around the coast!

The Dudley–Kingswinford line passed through a heavily mined area where coal and fireclay were extracted in abundance. It was therefore not surprising that subsidence was a problem, especially in the vicinity of Pensnett. This caused operational disruptions on the line. Typical were delays which began on 13 October 1924, when Lenches Bridge was closed for repairs; a shuttle tram service to and from each side of the bridge being operated. It therefore came as little surprise that the Dudley–Kingswinford line was the first of the D&SDET's routes to close, which it did on Thursday, 31 December 1925.

A Kingswinford tram works through Dudley Market Place. The service operated from the sidings there and as the Conductor is on the front balcony this is probably a car entering service. This is a detail from a coloured postcard, which explains the image's somewhat hand-drawn appearance! *(Author's Collection)*

There are remarkably few photographs showing anything of the Dudley–Kingswinford line before its destination. This is therefore quite a rarity – and a bit of a fluke! A photograph of a parade by Pensnett Primitive Methodist Sunday School – possibly their anniversary one – passing the Church of St Mark, behind the trees on the right. As the photograph is taken a gust of wind blew back a banner and revealed a heavily laden Dudley-bound Kingswinford car! *(Author's Collection)*

High Oak, Pensnett, showing the Dudley–Kingswinford tramlines and overhead. Together with the above image, this is all that is known of to show anything of the line before its terminus. There is a passing loop by the junction with Commonside (left), which is where the usefully scribed 'X' is! *(Peter Glew's Collection)*

The junction between High Street and Summerhill, Kingswinford, is a staggered crossroads. Seen from the latter, the Dudley–Kingswinford tramlines swung first right then left and they crossed between the two. The milk churns on the left are a reminder of a service provided by the KLR of collecting milk from farms along its way and delivering them to other points on the system. *(Author's Collection)*

Looking back towards The Cross, Kingswinford from Summerhill, c. 1924. A lady is in the waiting room but the car is further up the line with the crew standing alongside it. In practice the cars tended to wait at this point. *(Author's Collection)*

In this detail from the previous photograph, note the white 'cone' on the traction pole above the bus. These were spotlights and to be found at all of the system's termini. They lit up a portion of the overhead at night to make things easier for the Conductors when swinging the trolley pole! The car is No. 65, a rebuilt City of Birmingham Tramways cable car and the competitor is a 'Grey Bus'. *(Author's Collection)*

A general view of the Kingswinford tram terminus in Summerhill. In the foreground the track can be seen sweeping in over The Cross from High Street. It ran a little distance up Summerhill, more or less to where the road narrowed. *(Author's Collection)*

A detail showing the waiting room arrangements at Summerhill tram terminus in Kingswinford. The Waiting Room was an old tramcar body, through the door of which a pair of men's folded legs can be seen. There is a pair of the dummy clock faces, presumably indicating the next departures to Dudley and Stourbridge. Alongside the Waiting Room is Fellows's Tea Rooms – Summerhill Refreshments, where they also sold ices. There are three boys in view, the middle one of which appears to be a Tramway Conductor, which suggests that this image is from during the Great War. *(Author's Collection)*

The first of two details from the previous photograph. This one shows the track arrangement at the terminus. The line from The Cross ran through to the terminal stub, off which there was a siding which ran back parallel to main line. In practice, however, it is believed that this was little used. *(Author's Collection)*

Car No. 38 at The Cross, Kingswinford in 1904, one of six cars fitted with covers similar to the improved designs by C.R. Bellamy, the General Manager of Liverpool Corporation Tramways. These entered service in April 1904 and, given cleanliness of the car and the leaves on the tree behind, this can't have been taken much later on. Another clue is that the following year these covers were shortened to a four-window pattern which was the same length as the lower saloon windows. Electric headlights were also fitted at the same time. *(Peter Glews Collection)*

A postcard which was sold at the time of the withdrawal of the Dudley–Kingswinford service in December 1925 with the caption 'The Last Tram between Kingswinford and Dudley – 31st December 1925'. Clearly this is not so: the tree behind is in leaf and the Conductor has the summer white top on his cap. It later emerged that the postcard was a souvenir, quickly produced by a local photographer who wrote the above words on a negative he had in stock! *(Author's Collection)*

6

KINGSWINFORD TO STOURBRIDGE VIA WORDSLEY

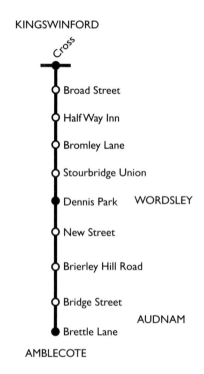

KINGSWINFORD

Cross

Broad Street

Half Way Inn

Bromley Lane

Stourbridge Union

Dennis Park   WORDSLEY

New Street

Brierley Hill Road

Bridge Street

AUDNAM

Brettle Lane

AMBLECOTE

L ike the other lines, work on construction of the Wordsley section of the Kingswinford–Stourbridge via Wordsley line had begun several weeks before the Dudley–Stourbridge main line opened on 26 July 1899. It opened on Monday, 7 December 1900 with a service frequency of every fifteen, twenty or thirty minutes. On 17 January 1901, the D&SDET instituted a through half-hourly service from Dudley to Stourbridge, via Pensnett, Kingswinford and Wordsley, so avoiding passengers having to change at Kingswinford.

In marked contrast to the line from Dudley, that to Stourbridge is reasonably level. From the Summerhill terminus it curves right into Market Street, which is built up on both sides as far as the junction with Park Street on the right. Past the Post Office, the left-hand side is undeveloped until after the junction with Broad Street on the right, at the end of a passing loop, where there are two substantial houses – Greenfield House and The Beeches.

Now, for a long stretch, there are a few buildings on either side as Market Street becomes Portway. A passing loop just before a malthouse on the left is at Halfway. Open land then on either side until a passing loop by the junction with Bromley Lane on the left. Past The Cedars (right) and The Stream and Stream Farm (left) there is another passing loop alongside the Stourbridge Union Workhouse (later Wordsley Hospital). On towards Wordsley, there is a passing loop opposite Sandfield Lodge on the right, this side being very built up, in contrast to the left-hand one. This continues to the junction with Wordsley Green on the right. A passing loop straddles this, opposite The Old Cat Inn.

From here the line descends more sharply, passing shops, houses and the Post Office on the right and the Church of the Holy Trinity on the left. Down the bank, passing the School of Art on the left, is an imposing building erected to train workers in the local glass industry in the decorative arts. A passing loop is entered at the foot of the bank, opposite The Rose & Crown Inn; the loop finishing by the junction with Brewery Street on the left.

The line then rises again, ascending to crown the Stourbridge Canal. There are a number of glassworks in this vicinity, whose cones are a distinctive sight, especially at night. After crossing the canal there is another passing loop. A wait here affords views of glassworks left and right, one of the former being the Red House Glassworks of Stuart & Sons. On downward again with housing on either side – this is Camp Hill. Then there is another passing loop, with, on the left, a school on the corner of Brook Street.

A little beyond the loop, the line crosses the Audnam Brook, the boundary between Wordsley and Audnam. Rising once more cars pass housing on the right and the Audnam Glassworks on the left followed almost immediately by Audnam House and its spacious grounds. Past the road named Stewkins on the right there is a final passing loop before the line joins the main Dudley–Stourbridge one just past the end of Brettell Lane, opposite The White Horse Inn on the left.

Soon after the closure of the Dudley–Kingswinford line on 31 December 1925, the future of the Kingswinford–Stourbridge one was placed in jeopardy. The service was cut back from 16 January 1926 and from 1 February the BMMO increased its bus services between the two towns. The end came in a little more than two months, the line closing on Saturday, 10 April 1926.

The view from Summerhill towards High Street (left) and Market Street (right), the start of the Kingswinford–Stourbridge line. People, and a dog, seem to be looking for something in the road! The tramlines forming the junction between the 'from Dudley' and 'to Stourbridge' lines can also be clearly seen. *(Author's Collection)*

A clearer view of the corner between High Street (left) and Market Street (right) showing the Kingswinford–Stourbridge line curving from the Summerhill terminus; an image assembled from a broken glass negative. *(Author's Collection)*

Market Street, Kingswinford, looking towards The Cross, taken from the passing loop next to The Swan Inn, which gives an excellent idea of what the Kingswinford–Stourbridge line looked like. Note the overhead wires suspended from span wires. The bakers' boy is standing in front of 'Ten Cottage Row', so called because there were ten cottages in a row! (*Author's Collection*)

There are no images of the Kingswinford–Stourbridge line between the previous photograph and the one above. The passing loop straddling the junction with Wordsley Green (right) and High Street is in the foreground, with the historic Old Cat Inn on the corner. (*Author's Collection*)

Wordsley War Memorial was unveiled on 12 November 1921. It stands on High Street in front of the Church of the Holy Trinity. Behind the children Wordsley Post Office can be seen and, above, the tramway overhead. In 2008, the name of Private Joseph Bateman, who was shot at dawn for desertion in December 1917, was added to the memorial, in the niche at the base of the metal plaque seen here. (*Author's Collection*)

Wordsley Post Office again (extreme left) in this view looking back up High Street towards Kingswinford. The tramway overhead was still suspended on span wires at this point. *(Author's Collection)*

The Wordsley School of Art (left) opened in 1899 following a campaign by local glass manufacturers to educate their employees and improve products to meet growing international competition. A matching half of the building (right of the main entrance in this view) was opened in 1909 to cater for the increasing demands for its services. The first instructor at the school was Frederick Carder (1863–1963) who designed the terracotta panels on the façade. Sadly these were stolen in 1993 and the building was demolished in 2001. In the distance a tramcar is working towards Amblecote. *(Author's Collection)*

A passing loop straddled the junction with Brewery Street (on the left here), before the Stourbridge–Kingswinford line began to climb towards the Stourbridge Canal. *(Author's Collection)*

Car No. 23 is about to cross the Audnam Brook, the boundary between Wordsley and Audnam, on its journey to Kingswinford. It was the first in a batch of sixteen similar cars which went into service in 1901. Alterations known to have been made to the car would date this to not before 1905 but also not much past that year. This is the clearest view of any part of the Kingswinford–Stourbridge line and rich in detail. The Red House glass cone is immediately above the tramcar. It is the sole survivor of over twenty such cones which once stood in this vicinity. *(Author's Collection)*

Audnam, looking towards Wordsley, close to the junction of the Kingswinford–Stourbridge line with the main Dudley–Stourbridge one at the foot of Brettell Lane, showing the first passing loop after the main line junction. Fashions suggest an early 1920s date for this image, the poster for the Scala Cinema, Stourbridge, reinforces this – it first opened its doors on 11 October 1920. *(www.stourbridge.com)*

The start of the same passing loop seen above is in the foreground of this view from Audnam looking towards High Street, Amblecote. Car No. 28 is heading in the direction of Kingswinford but showing 'DUDLEY' on its destination blind! The '25' on the traction pole denotes a fare stage number. *(www.stourbridge.com)*

Looking from the Kingswinford–Stourbridge line down High Street, Amblecote. The main Dudley–Stourbridge line junction can be seen swinging in from the left, as can the start of the long double track section down to The Fish. The lack of overhead wires above the Kingswinford tracks suggests that this photograph was taken after this line had closed. Typically the overhead wires were removed fairly soon after a tramway ceased operation but the tracks often remained in the road for some years. (*Author's Collection*)

The other end of the long double track section up Amblecote High Street, which began just after the junction with Collis Street (left) and Wollaston Road (right). A Kingswinford-bound car, possibly No.38, has the original five-window pattern of 'Bellamy' top cover fitted, which dates the photograph to between 1904 and 1905. The 'PRIORY TEA' advert is carried on the roof of a KLR tram waiting outside The Fish Inn. To the right a sign writer is painting something on the wall of The Little Pig Inn. (*Author's Collection*)

7

THE KINVER
LIGHT RAILWAY

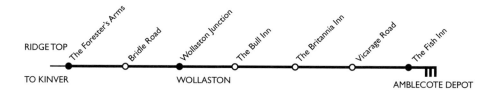

RIDGE TOP   The Forester's Arms   Bridle Road   Wollaston Junction   The Bull Inn   The Britannia Inn   Vicarage Road   The Fish Inn

TO KINVER   WOLLASTON   AMBLECOTE DEPOT

The Kinver Light Railway (KLR) was promoted by the D&SDET's parent company – the BET Co. – as the Kinver Light Railway Order, 1898, which was approved by the Board of Trade on 7 March 1899. Construction began immediately, the first 1 mile 15 chain section from Coalbournbrook via Wollaston Road; High Street Wollaston and Bridgnorth Road to The Ridge was a conventional grooved rail street tramway; the second 1 mile 32 chain section was laid on the grass verge alongside the main Stourbridge to Bridgnorth road using Vignoles (non-grooved 'bullhead') rail on wooden sleepers with grooved rail used only on the curves. This latter construction was also used on the final 1 mile 48 chain private right-of-way section, which was entirely protected by fencing and the hardest to construct, necessitating building half a dozen bridges across the river and canal, and a depôt to accommodate eight cars for summer traffic, on marshy ground in Hyde Meadow. This final section, along with the roadside one, shared the KLR's unique feature of wooden traction poles, said to blend in with the rural environment!

All was ready by late March 1901, and the KLR was inspected by the Board of Trade on an inauspicious date – Monday, 1 April 1901! The inspector's report imposed serious restrictions on the KLR's planned operation. Doubts were expressed on the suitability of tramcar wheels for running on Vignoles rail, resulting in an overall 10 mph speed limit being imposed and the lack of signalling at passing loops resulted in a ban on the KLR's operation at night. Furthermore, the use of single-decked bogie cars alone was recommended, owing to the tightness of some of the curves where, it was feared, double-deckers might derail. This was especially unfortunate as three new such cars had been ordered. Undaunted, the KLR opened on Friday, 5 April 1901, which was also Good Friday. It rained heavily all day but this did not deter over 14,000 people from travelling to Kinver by this novel form of transport.

In the spring of 1902, three open-sided trams were delivered; eight-wheel bogie cars, which could seat 56. At each end of the cars was an enclosed portion which could seat 12 people, 6 a side facing each other; another 32 could be seated on eight cross seats, four abreast. Again, these cars could be overloaded and regularly carried 75-80 people. Like the cut-down double-deckers, when delivered they were painted in a chocolate livery. These cars proved very popular for outings, such as on 2 August 1902 when Wollaston Primitive Methodist Sunday School annual treat saw 200 children, teachers and friends go by Kinver special tramcars and then walk to and from Kinver Edge.

The KLR proved a great success through a combination of a half-hourly service and low fares – 3*d* for the whole journey. By 1904 the KLR had proved so popular that the tramway company decided to double sections of the line. Ideally they would have liked to double along its entire length, but restrictions such as the roadside section through Stourton, and the sheer cost of purchasing all of the land required, restricted this to two main sections: between The Fish and The Ridge Top through Wollaston and between Hyde Park stop and Kinver Station. George Law & Co. of Kidderminster again did the work. On 1 April 1905, Stourbridge Council's Highways & Improvements Committee stated that: 'The surveyor reported that the Tramway Company commenced doubling the track within the area at Wollaston, as sanctioned by the Council and had broken up the road in several places along the route.' On 6 May 1905, the surveyor reported that: 'the doubling of the Tramway track within the Council's area was completed as far as Bridle Road by Easter', and on 3 June 1905, he reported that: 'The doubling of the Tramway Track was nearly completed'; the section of the KLR between Hyde Park and Kinver being doubled in 1906.

The KLR was always popular, particularly in the 'summer' (Easter to October) months when Kinver Depot opened to deal with the increased traffic.

A through service from Birmingham–Smethwick–Dudley–Brierley Hill–Kinver was run on several days a week.

The KLR survived the Great War unscathed, seeing a great increase in its goods traffic, and had new combination open and closed cars, similar to Australian designs, built for it in 1916. But, by the mid-1920s, a combination of motorbus competition, the need for major track replacement and ever worsening financial results had nibbled away much of the Black Country tramway system, fewer and fewer through services operated and the connecting lines closed. Its last full year was 1929, when the summer, excursion and special services all operated. That autumn, Kinver Depot closed for the last time. The KLR reverted to its basic winter service of one car each morning and evening weekdays, and a morning and lunchtime car on Saturdays, but no Sunday service. At the end of January 1930, the tramway company stated that they wanted to abandon the remaining tramway services as soon as possible. They reached agreement with Dudley, Stourbridge, Amblecote and Brierley Hill councils, and the KLR closed on Saturday, 8 February 1930. The replacement Midland Red omnibus service worked from Stourbridge, via Wollaston and the Stewponey, to Kinver over the ordinary main roads.

The full story of the KLR is told in the companion volume to this book: *The Kinver Light Railway: Echoes of a Lost Tramway.*

SUMMER TIME TABLE.
DUDLEY STATION and FISH INN for KINVER.

WEEK DAYS,

Leave Dudley Station at 5.15 a.m.. and every 15 minutes until 1 p m., then every 8 and 10 minutes until 8.30 p.m, then every 15 minutes until 10.45 p.m.

Leave Fish Inn at 5.30 a.m., and every 15 minutes until 1.5 p.m., then every 8 and 10 minutes until 8.30 p.m, then every fifteen minutes until 10.50 p.m.

SATURDAYS.

Leave Dudley Station at 5.15, a.m., and every fifteen minutes until 8 20 a.m., then every ten minutes until 1.0 p.m. then every six and seven minutes until 10.50 p.m.

Leave Fish Inn at 5.30 a.m., and every fifteen minutes until 8.20 a.m , then every ten minutes until 1.5 p.m., then every six and seven minutes until 10.50 p.m.

SUNDAYS,

LEAVE DUDLEY STATION at 10.0 a.m. and every 15 minutes until 1.0 p.m., then every 8 minutes until 10.20 p.m.

LEAVE FISH INN, at 10.5 a.m., and every 15 minutes until 1.20 p.m , then every 8 minutes until 10.30 p.m.

SUMMER TIME TABLE.
FISH INN and KINVER.

FROM FISH INN To KINVER.	Week Days.	FROM KINVER To FISH INN.
6.0 a.m.		5.30 a.m.
7.0 ,,		6.30 ,,
8.0 ,,		7.25 ,,
8.55 ,,		8.30 ,,
9.45 ,,		9.20 ,,
10.35 ,,		10.10 ,,
11.25 ,,		11.0 ,,
12.15 p.m.		11.50 ,,
1.5 ,,		12.40 p.m.
1.30 ,,		1.30 ,,
		1.55 ,,
and every 25 minutes until		and every 25 minutes until
8.35 p.m.		9.0 p.m.
9.25 ,,		9.50 ,,
10.15 ,,		10.40 ,,
11.5 ,,		

Sundays.

Leave FISH INN for KINVER at 9.25 a.m. and every 25 minutes until 9.30 p.m., then 10.0 and 10.30 p.m.

Leave KINVER for FISH INN at 9.0 a.m., and every 25 minutes until 10.0 p.m.

The summer timetable for the KLR from 1904 giving (left) the times to and from Dudley and (right) those from The Fish Inn – the line's one terminus – to Kinver. *(Author's Collection)*

The mainstay of the KLR service all year round were the 'Cradley bogie' cars, such as No. 58, seen here in the yard at Amblecote Depot in 1921. These 52-seater cars had a five-window non-smoking centre section, screened by bulkhead doors, which can be seen in this view. *(Author's Collection)*

Since the publication of the companion volume to this book – *The Kinver Light Railway: Echoes of a Lost Tramway* – some readers have kindly forwarded copies of photographs unavailable at the time of writing. One such is this very detailed view inside the power house at Amblecote Depot, which is dated 20 May 1929. *(Courtesy of Trevor Hartley)*

A detail from the previous photograph that shows switchgear labelled 'SPRINGSMIRE' and 'STEWPONEY' *(Courtesy of Trevor Hartley)*

A version of this well-known postcard view of The Ridge Top was reproduced on page 50 of *The Kinver Light Railway: Echoes of a Lost Tramway* but this version is a lot clearer. Looking back towards The Forester's Arms on the county boundary between Worcestershire and Staffordshire and the point at which the KLR began to move to the side of the road. *(Peter Glews Collection)*

In another detail from the same photograph, the KLR line can be seen sweeping over from the middle of the road to its left-hand side before occupying the verge down the road to The Stewponey. *(Peter Glews Collection)*

A small portion of this photograph was reproduced on page 60 of *The Kinver Light Railway: Echoes of a Lost Tramway*. The KLR line can be seen swinging across the then staggered crossroads forming the junction between the 'from Kidderminster' and the 'from Wolverhampton' sections of the road that is now the A449. Isaac Elwell's tenure of The Stewponey & Foley Arms Hotel was over and the hostelry had passed to Henry Berry. *(Author's Collection)*

A version of this early 1900s view showing Car No. 51 was reproduced on page 81 of *The Kinver Light Railway: Echoes of a Lost Tramway*. This version is more complete and sharper. The shot was clearly posed; as the Motorman and Conductor look out while a lady with a small girl make their way from the car. Behind the fence the KLR's long waiting shelter can be seen. *(Author's Collection)*

'Cradley bogie' car No. 58 stands empty within the KLR's Kinver Station. Between 1924 and 1925 the eight cars of this kind were rebuilt to create a design of FRONT EXIT CAR and it was upgraded with upholstered seating, including arm rests. Behind the car the side of the Kinver Station's booking office can be seen. *(Author's Collection)*

No other image more adequately conveys an impression of just how popular and busy the KLR was than this view, which is a detail from an image reproduced on page 87 of *The Kinver Light Railway: Echoes of a Lost Tramway*. This is the buffer stop end of the Kinver Station, with all three concentric lines full of cars! *(Author's Collection)*

The Birmingham & District Tramways.

Guide to Kinver.

VICARAGE VIEW TEA ROOMS, KINVER.	Manageress : Mrs. MARY WELLS.

DINNERS, TEAS & LUNCHEONS.　　**The Best in Kinver.**　　Charges Strictly Moderate.

TEAS, with Bread & Butter, various kinds of Cake, Preserves, Marmalade & Salads, 9d. each
Ditto, with 2 Eggs, 1/- Ditto, with Boiled Ham, 1/2. Ditto, with Ham (English) & Eggs, 1/3 to 1/6

Workmen's and Children's Parties a Speciality.　　For Large Parties a Reduction from above prices
Accommodation for 600. Large Field of 4 Acres for Sport, &c. All kinds of Mineral Waters, Hop Ale, &c
Cycles Stored and Tickets given.

JOHN PRICE & SONS, PRINTERS, BILSTON. TEL. 106.

Kinver was widely promoted by local tramway companies, some of whom produced illustrated guides, such as this one by the Birmingham & District Tramways, which again came to light after publication of *The Kinver Light Railway: Echoes of a Lost Tramway. (Author's Collection)*

How many people who visited Kinver via the KLR bought souvenir postcards such as this one showing one of the rock houses on Holy Austin Rock? In recent years the houses have been refurbished and are opened to the public by the National Trust. *(Author's Collection)*

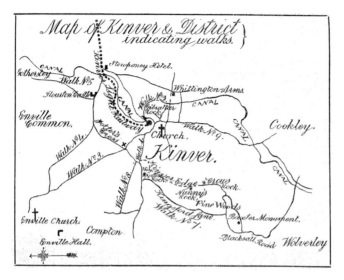

One of the tramway company guides to Kinver included a series of eight walks of varying length and difficulty, which the more adventurous of the KLR's passengers were entreated to try. *(Author's Collection)*

From the same guide here is the itinerary of Walk No. 5 to Gothersley and back – a distance of four miles. The juxtaposition of the advertisements is probably no accident – a decent tea would be a just reward after this walk! *(Author's Collection)*

ILLUSTRATED GUIDE TO KINVER.

Compa Cottage Holiday Home and Tea Gardens.
Accommodation for Large or Small Parties ; Terms Moderate.
Apartments with Board from 15/- to £1 per week. Week-ends
from 3/- Agent for the Cycle Touring Club; covered accom-
modation for 200.   TRY OUR NINEPENNY TEAS.
G. MARTINDALE, Proprietor.

WALK No. 5.
Gothersley—4 miles.

The tram should be taken to "The Stewpony" as in Walk 4, and then one can take one of two routes, either by the Canal side or by the Road.   The latter forms one of the most delightful walks in the district, the whole of the distance being covered by well-wooded country which affords welcome shade, whilst every now and then a charming prospect is afforded by a glimpse of many old-time English homesteads, situated among rustic scenery and interspersed here and there with various brooklets.

Towards the end of the journey will be found a one-time seat of industry known as "Green's Forge," and hard by refreshment can be obtained at the quaint old Hostelry, the "Navigation," which vies with the Whittington Inn, previously mentioned in point of age.

The return journey may be made by the Canal side, and this is recommended, as the walk is extremely picturesque and interesting.

The scenery is equally charming, and if required, the walk can be extended when arriving back at the "Navigation" by a ramble across Highgate Common, which is a large expanse of bracken and verdure-covered country, abounding in animal and bird life.

THOMPSON   **Electrical Light & Power Engineers**
AND   Private Installations, Bells, Telephones,
and Works Equipment.
PASFIELD. 20. High St.. Stourbridge.

Stourton Castle.

Advertised above and seen here is Martindale's Tea Gardens, which, as the advertisement said, could provide covered accommodation for 200. What did you get for the 'Ninepenny Tea' though? *(Author's Collection)*

8

THE STOURBRIDGE
HIGH STREET EXTENSION

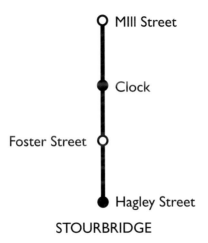

MIll Street

Clock

Foster Street

Hagley Street

STOURBRIDGE

Proposals to extend the Stourbridge end of the Dudley–Stourbridge line up through Lower and (Upper) High Street were contained in the Dudley & District Light Railways Order 1898, which was eventually granted on 1 November 1898. The track work for the extension was completed by the end of 1900, but Stourbridge Council and the D&SDET could not agree over the type of overhead pole to be erected. Once settled, the contract for the electrical equipment was placed with George Hill & Co. It was stated in April 1901 that the trams were expected to be running in about ten weeks' time and two weeks later, on 17 April 1901, the AGM of the D&SDET was informed that the line through Stourbridge High Street was nearly complete, and would be 'opened within a few weeks.' Col. Yorke of the Board of Trade inspected that line on 4 July 1901 and it opened for traffic on 3 September 1901.

From the main line's original terminus opposite the Stourbridge Town Goods Station by Mill Street the extension line crosses over the River Stour, the boundary between Staffordshire and Worcestershire and between Amblecote and Stourbridge. Immediately before this a pair of railway lines from the Goods Station cross the tramway tracks on the level; necessitating notches to have been cut in the tramlines to permit the railway wheel flanges to pass over. Stourbridge Road becomes Lower High Street once the Stour is crossed and from here both sides of the line are solidly built up. Mill Street itself is passed on the left. Beyond is the imposing range of Turney's Leather & Parchment works, where sheepskin is turned into parchment, used in vast quantities for legal documents such as deeds, leases and mortgages. The street is on a rising gradient and just past the Congregational and Presbyterian chapels, which face each other across the street, a long section of double track is entered, characterised by centre traction poles with elaborate side arm brackets. This section ends opposite King Edward VI Grammar School, established in 1552. The rising gradient levels out just past the junctions with Coventry Street (on the left) and Drury Lane (on the right). There is a stop opposite Stourbridge's Town Clock, which has a pair of faces pointing up and down the street. Its mechanism is housed within the Town and Market Hall of 1832 and the hands are driven by a shaft. Here, Lower High Street becomes (Upper) High Street, although locally no one uses the 'Upper'. Owing to opposition from Stourbridge Council, from this point onwards the line takes on a most unusual character. It is double track, but with the lines almost in the gutter. In addition, the entire road surface is paved with wooden blocks! This was a concession made to lessen the noise made by the trams. However, as they did not use the road surface at all, and are steel tyred vehicles running on steel rails just as everywhere else, it makes no difference! There are no stops in this section between the Town Clock and Foster Street. At this point, the line to The Lye branches off. Its junction is operationally awkward. Cars bound for The Lye need to run past Foster Street and then reverse, taking a single right-hand curve into the street. High Street cars ran past this point, where another unusual feature could be seen. Here the street is narrow and there was not room to erect traction poles to support the overhead wires. So, special plates – called rosettes – were attached to points on opposing buildings and span wires were strung across to support the overhead wires. Approaching the junction with New Road on the right, the double track converges into a single line and runs in the centre of the road past, on the left, the Free Library & Art & Technical Institute, Swan Inn and terminates opposite the County Court building.

Almost immediately upon opening there were complaints about the congestion the trams caused in the narrow High Street, shopkeepers said that customers' carriages could only be left outside their shops for a very short time before a tram would come through and the carriage would have to be moved out of the way; in addition, they had not sufficient time between trams to load or unload their goods. The D&SDET, however, also complained that its cars were so delayed by other vehicles standing in the High Street that the service was disorganised. After a few weeks only, the service was temporarily cut back to the Town Clock.

The situation had been created by Stourbridge Council. The D&SDET had originally intended to lay a single track through the very narrow street. However, Stourbridge UDC insisted on having a double line with tracks laid against each kerb; also that there should be a twenty-minute service only and that there should not be two tramcars in the High Street between the Clock and Foster Street at one and the same time. In addition, the Council specified that the whole width and length of the street from the Clock onwards should be paved with wooden blocks – and not just any kind of wood either but Jarrah, which was only available as an import from Australia! Of course, this was nonsense as steel-tyred tram wheels running on steel tramlines make their own kind of noise, whatever the road is paved with!

It seems that the D&SDET had not originally intended the proposed single track through High Street for passenger service, but only as a connecting link with the new route to Lye and Hayes, to be built under the 1900 Order; this line was to make a left-hand trailing connection at Foster Street, near the far end of High Street. On 4 November 1901, the service began to run through the High Street once more, but the D&SDET found that it was impossible to run a tram from the centre of the town to the top of the town and back again in time to fit in with the regular service; the through service had, therefore, been withdrawn. In response, the D&SDET proposed that two trams should be allowed to pass each other in the street, otherwise the Company was not prepared to run through.

The Company had spent a great deal of money to try to satisfy the Council, but when it came to try to work the service the agreement was such that it was incapable of being carried out to the letter. Early in December 1901, however, the D&SDET claimed to have been running a ten-minute service while keeping to the agreement not to allow two cars to pass. The main line service continued to run through to the terminus near the County Court, although a great many complaints continued to be received regarding congestion in the (Upper) High Street – both from the D&SDET and the general public. Requests from Kingswinford for a through service to Stourbridge met with the Company's reply that it could not see its way to do this, owing to the restriction the Council had seen fit to impose on tramway traffic through High Street.

Some resolution of these matters came with the establishment of a terminus for the services to Dudley and Kingswinford in the centre of the High Street, just past the Town Clock, by the junction of Coventry and Markey streets.

Here, outside The Old Bank at Fare Stage 24, became the main loading place for the above services; the line through (Upper) High Street effectively becoming a shuttle service to the Hagley Road terminus and the means of cars bound for The Lye gaining access to that line.

Slightly down the line, in Lower High Street, the D&SDET resolved to double the track from Scotland House, just below the Enville Street junction, down to the foot of the hill at Mill Street. Some Stourbridge Councillors wanted to make, as a condition of agreeing to this improvement, a proviso that the Company should then operate the Kingswinford cars right through to Stourbridge terminus. The Company claimed that this was not possible, owing to the restriction which the Council had imposed on traffic through the (Upper) High Street, and the Council did not press the point further. The Stourbridge Lower High Street section of double line was completed by the beginning of December 1903. The bottom of Lower High Street is very low and close to the River Stour. It is, therefore, very prone to flooding after heavy rain, and so the D&SDET agreed with the Council to put drain boxes in the new tracks laid at this point.

During track relaying along the Dudley–Stourbridge main line early in 1925, the opportunity was taken to rationalise the track in (Upper) High Street, Stourbridge. Apart from to gain access to The Lye route, the tracks saw little use, and the right-hand set, when looking up the street with the Town Clock behind, seldom saw any use. After rationalisation the track used to gain The Lye line was cut back to a car's length beyond the trailing points into Foster Street and the other line was cut back to two–three cars' lengths past the junction with Market Street. Cars no longer ran to the County Court terminus in Hagley Road.

Despite the DS&DET's investment in Stourbridge, local people were often critical of the tramway service. Typical is this comment on 20 May 1912, when, at a meeting of Stourbridge Council the Chairman said:

> ... there was no part of the tramway system which was treated so badly as Stourbridge. At holiday times people for the most part shunned coming via Stourbridge to Kinver simply because they were landed at High Street, Wollaston, and sometimes had to stop there two or three hours before they could get to Kinver. He saw no reason why the company should not run a few trams from Enville Street to Kinver (hear, hear). It was a nuisance to people coming from Birmingham to find themselves landed at Wollaston until a car came along on which there was some spare room. Sometimes they got on at Wollaston and rode down to the Fish in order to retain their seat to come back, but the company tried to avoid that by running straight through Wollaston on the home journey.

The Stourbridge High Street Extension line closed with the rest of the Dudley–Stourbridge main line on Saturday, 1 March 1930, the last departure being car No. 23 at 23.00. The following day a full service of Midland Red buses, operated by the BMMO, replaced the trams and a new through service from Wednesbury via Tipton, Dudley and Brierley Hill was introduced.

Before the trams came – Stourbridge High Street, c. 1880. It would be another four years before D&SST steam trams linked the town to Dudley and another twenty-one years before DS&DET electric trams ran through the High Street. Stourbridge's town clock was installed in 1857 and made at the Stourbridge Ironworks to designs by engineer William Millward. Its mechanism was housed within the Market Hall and the hands were moved via a drive shaft, which can be seen here. *(Author's Collection)*

For just over a quarter of a century, the Woolpack Inn was probably the closest hostelry to Stourbridge's tram terminus, and had much patronage to lose when the Dudley–Stourbridge line was extended. Perhaps the 'Trams pass the door' footnote is therefore a little prophetic? However, maybe the house's reputation for tripe buoyed trade. *(Author's Collection)*

Mrs.

E. Dalloway,

WOOLPACK

INN,

Stourbridge .

Celebrated
HOME BREWED ALES

Finest quality
WINES and SPIRITS.

Noted Tripe House
for over half-a-century.

Trams pass the door.

Lower High Street, Stourbridge, 1925: Mrs Dalloway's pub can be seen at the extreme left. This is a good view of the start of the High Street Extension line and shows the point where the single line became double track. The impressive building in front of the delivery van was built by John Bradley (1769–1816), the iron founder, in the early nineteenth century in the then popular 'Strawberry Hill Gothic' style. *(www.stourbridge.com)*

One problem the DS&DET had to face after it extended its Dudley–Stourbridge line through the centre of Stourbridge was the fact that the River Stour was prone to bursting its banks and flooding the bottom of Lower High Street. Here is just one instance. The parapets of the bridge over the river from which the town derives its name can be seen clearly on each side. *(Author's Collection)*

A regular sufferer from the Stour flooding the bottom of Stourbridge was the Town Station. This is the canal-to-rail transhipment shed and warehouse that used to stand at the centre of the goods station, which opened on 1 January 1880. The last train to leave the station departed on 30 April 1965, and all work officially ceased at the yard on 5 July 1965, although the line remained open until 20 September 1965. The track was lifted by October 1967 and this photograph was taken shortly afterwards. *(Neil Pitts/Author's Collection)*

Flooding in Stourbridge Town Goods Station in the early 1920s. The large mill-like building on the right was the works of William J. Turney & Co., who were parchment and leather producers. *(Author's Collection)*

So bad were the floods in Stourbridge that postcards were produced to 'commemorate' them, such as this one recording those on 1 June 1924. This seems to have caused a lot of damage to the road and almost certainly disrupted the tramway service for some time. *(Author's Collection)*

Another view of the 1 June 1924 flooding in Lower High Street, Stourbridge. The tramway must be at least two feet below the water level at this point judging by where it is in relation to the shop fronts. In the distance a small crowd beneath umbrellas survey the scene. *(History of Wollaston Group)*

Stourbridge-bound standard Car No. 28 almost has a bow wave! Was it moving through all this water? Due to the way electric tramways were wired – positive from the overhead wire; negative return via the track – they could work through water! *(Author's Collection)*

LOWER HIGH STREET, STOURBRIDGE, P. 825.

On a drier occasion this view shows a look back down Lower High Street towards the flooded area seen above and the start of the High Street Extension Line. Lunt's coal cart is parked in front of the former Congregational Chapel. Breeze – named on the cart – is very small coal used on hearths such as those used by chain and nail makers. *(Author's Collection)*

A splendidly detailed view from around 1920 of the top part of Lower High Street, Stourbridge showing the original frontage of King Edward VI Grammar School, which was founded in 1552. The centre traction poles were very elaborately decorated with scroll bracket work. Either the photographer chose the right moment or the street was remarkably quiet! *(Author's Collection)*

A look back down Lower High Street, Stourbridge from about the point where the three men were standing in the previous photograph. This also shows the original Grammar School frontage to good effect. In the foreground the double track section of line is merging back into a single track. *(Author's Collection)*

A postcard view of King Edward VI Grammar School, Stourbridge which, for once, has managed to retain the tramway's overhead lines. The traction pole in the centre has the kind of guard protecting it usually seen around the base of trees in parks. *(Author's Collection)*

Only 50 feet of film is known showing DS&DET trams in Stourbridge. Taken by Stanley Eades on 26 May 1929, it includes a short sequence in Lower High Street, Stourbridge, showing people boarding a tramcar. Behind is DS&DET Car No. 5, which was restored and ran for twenty-six years at the Black Country Living Museum. *(Author's Collection)*

Lower High Street, Stourbridge is a rising gradient when travelling from Dudley; this is almost at its summit. The photograph is from the late 1920s. There are more cars on the road yet there is also a horse-drawn milk cart (left) and a handcart (right) over which there seems to be a bit of haggling! *(Author's Collection)*

The policeman on traffic duty is standing in the middle of the single track connecting Lower High Street with (Upper) High Street. To the left is the corner of Market Street and to the right that of Coventry Street. On that corner stands Nickolls & Perks, who have been wine merchants in Stourbridge since 1797. Their shop stands over vaults which date from the fifteenth century. *(Author's Collection)*

Another coloured postcard – no overhead wires – looking from the corner of Market Street, Stourbridge, at, if the Town Clock is to be believed, 10.20 one morning. The building to the right is the Old Bank. *(Author's Collection)*

Stourbridge Town Clock in the early 1900s. Overhead wires can be seen disappearing between Hilton's Booteries and the tailor's shop beyond it – this was the junction for the Enville Street line to Wollaston, which dates the photograph to later than December 1902, but probably not much after this date. *(Author's Collection)*

This view is from just within (Upper) High Street, Stourbridge and shows the point work where the single track from Lower High Street diverged into double track. The pattern created by the Jarrah-wood blocks which the street was paved with can be seen in the road. *(Author's Collection)*

A detail from the previous photograph identifying the tram as Car No. 37, which entered service early in 1901. *(Author's Collection)*

Isaac Nash Jnr, Chairman of Stourbridge Urban District Council, was implacably opposed to trams and their 'intrusion' into the High Street. He stymied the Dudley, Stourbridge & District Electric Tramways Bill of 1904, which would have seen their system expand. He also insisted both upon the (Upper) High Street tracks being widely spaced apart and the road surface being paved in Jarrah-wood blocks. So, how many wood blocks does it take to pave (Upper) High Street, Stourbridge? Here is the proof – 20,000! *(Author's Collection)*

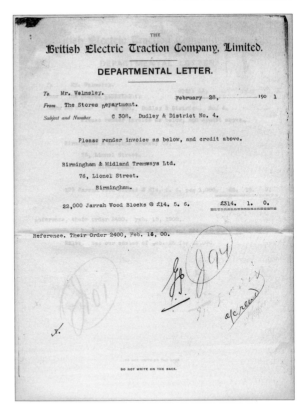

This view of the Town Clock shows its original clock face, which was replaced with a simpler design in the mid-1920s, and the terminus for the Dudley and Kingswinford services opposite the clock. On the right there is an impressive pile of shoeboxes in Warrilo's upper window! *(Author's Collection)*

105

A detail from the previous photograph showing the short-working arrangements in more detail. This point was Fare Stage 24 on the journey from Dudley. The two 'dummy' clock faces state: (top) FIRST CAR LEAVES FOR WORDSLEY KINGSWINFORD & PENSNETT AT and shows 11.45 and the (bottom) FIRST CAR LEAVES FOR BRIERLEY HILL & DUDLEY AT 12.05. *(Author's Collection)*

A very animated scene in the centre of Stourbridge High Street in the mid-1920s. Two men are arguing over something in the newspaper. Behind them is F.H. Alcock's store – he sold gramophone records and sheet music. The van to the right is from Parker, Winder & Achurch, a Birmingham ironmonger who became an electrical contractor. *(Author's Collection)*

Early in 1925 an opportunity was taken to rationalise the track in (Upper) High Street, Stourbridge. The terminus was drawn back from Hagley Road to just north of the line's junction with Market Street, outside Freeman, Hardy & Willis. That is a very impressive display in the one window of the CENTRAL HOTEL. *(Author's Collection)*

A view of DS&DET Car No. 23, which was withdrawn in 1919, seen standing at the position of the later cut-back terminus in High Street, Stourbridge. *(Author's Collection)*

107

Not much chance of getting a tram down Stourbridge High Street on this occasion, the details of which are unknown. One possibility is Empire Day – 24 May – which saw High Streets up and down the country bedecked with flags like this and during which processions of this kind were held. The photograph gives a good view of (Upper) High Street. *(Author's Collection)*

Continuing along (Upper) High Street, Stourbridge, both the Jarrah-wood blocks used to pave the road surface and the closeness of the lines to the kerb can be seen in this photograph showing DS&DET Car No. 38 waiting to depart for Kingswinford. By the traction pole (right) a window cleaner has parked his handcart, which is sufficient to have made it impossible for a tramcar to pass. *(Author's Collection)*

The points made in the previous photograph are also illustrated by this extract from the original plans for the High Street Extension – the black dots show the bases of traction poles. *(Author's Collection)*

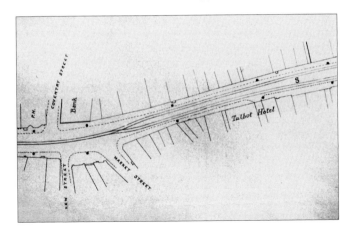

Midway along (Upper) High Street, Stourbridge, from just past the Post Office, emphasising the separation of the two lines along the road. On the right, just by where the man and lady are passing each other, was a passage leading to The Alhambra – Stourbridge's original theatre – which opened in February 1867. *(Author's Collection)*

Further up (Upper) High Street, Stourbridge, by its junction with Foster Street (right), where the line to The Lye branched off. Beneath the impressively large gas lamp (right) a newsvendor has set up his stall and a sign projecting from the lamp's standard directs people to the 'TOWN STATION'. *(Author's Collection)*

(Upper) High Street, Stourbridge, past its junction with St John's Road, looking towards the Free Library which opened in 1906. The original tram terminus was just a few yards on from this point. *(Author's Collection)*

Looking back at (Upper) High Street from Church Street with Bordeaux House in the background. The convergence of the tramlines can be seen centre left. On the right, a baker's boy is staring hard at the cameraman! *(Author's Collection)*

Another commercial postcard of the same view, which is franked 20 July 1908, showing a GWR bus setting out for Bromsgrove and making use of the tramline, around which the surface was better maintained than the rest of the road. *(Author's Collection)*

The GWR began its omnibus service between Stourbridge Town Station – seen here – and Bromsgrove, via Hagley, Clent and Belbroughton on 13 February 1905. It was worked by two Milnes-Daimler vehicles, both of which are in the photograph. *(Author's Collection)*

In 1916, the author's grandfather used the GWR's omnibus service to travel to Pedmore – and kept the ticket. Seen here is the reverse of the ticket, which listed the GWR's other ROAD MOTOR CARS. *(Author's Collection)*

Before 1904 this was the scene which greeted passengers as they approached the terminus of the Stourbridge High Street Extension Line – E. Roberts' Leather & Grindery Stores. Going by his signs, there was little Mr Roberts could not do to a shoe or a boot, from making them to measure, to any variety of repair. *(Author's Collection)*

Plans for a free library in Stourbridge were given a boost in 1902 when the philanthropist Andrew Carnegie, a great benefactor of public libraries across the English-speaking world, donated £3,000 out of the total £9,000 cost of construction. Building work began in February 1904, on the site of Robert's cobbler's shop at the junction of Hagley Road and Church Street. The reading and news rooms were opened on 1 August 1905, and the lending and reference department opened on 2 April 1906. The completed Free Library is seen here after 1908, when the clock tower (right) was added as a memorial to Isaac Nash Jnr. This also gives a very clear view of the convergence of the tramlines leading to the terminus. *(Author's Collection)*

The terminus of the Stourbridge High Street Extension line was outside the County Court building, which was erected in 1838. It is the one with the lady and the pram outside it in this view. *(Author's Collection)*

A major change outside Stourbridge's free library was the unveiling of the town's war memorial on 25 February 1923. It was the work of celebrated Manchester sculptor John Cassidy (1860–1939). *(Author's Collection)*

113

9

STOURBRIDGE TO
THE LYE & THE HAYES

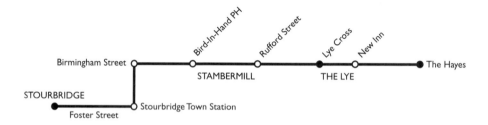

T he line between Stourbridge and The Lye was authorised with a number of road widenings and other improvements under the Dudley & District Light Railways (Extensions) Order, 1900, which was given its powers on 3 April 1900. The Lye line comprised three sections:

- from a junction with Railway No.4 of the 1898 Order in High Street, Stourbridge, along Foster Street to the junction of that street with Birmingham Street – 1 furlong 2.5 chains;
- from the above along Birmingham Street and Stourbridge Road, to The Cross, Lye – I mile and 7.5 chains, and;
- from the above continuing through High Street and (Upper) High Street, to terminate at the junction with Hayes Lane at The Hayes – 5 furlongs 1.6 chains.

Track laying was almost completed on the Lye line by the beginning of July 1902 in spite of bad weather and difficulties due to the road widening entailed.

The line was eventually completed by about the end of August and the Board of Trade Inspection was carried out by Colonel von Donop on 2 October 1902. However, it took several weeks for the approval to come through and the line was not opened to traffic until Saturday, 1 November 1902. However, for a short time cars could only operate as far as Lye Cross, as a lamp at that point had yet to be re-sited to give sufficient clearance for the cars! The opening day was a very busy one, owing to the combination of the Lye Wakes holiday that weekend, fine weather and the novelty of the trams, which ran a ten minutes' service. Thereafter, the cars ran every five, ten or thirty minutes, with variations; the service being operated from the D&SDET's Amblecote depot.

From its awkward junction with the Stourbridge High Street extension line, the route to The Lye traverses Foster Street, passing Stourbridge Town Station and beneath the railway lines serving Stourbridge Town Goods Station. Here the road becomes Foster Street East and its improvement was at the expense of the tramway company to facilitate the construction and operation of the line. Past St John's School on the corner of Angel Street on the left and Mount Street on the right, then down a dip to swing right into Birmingham Street.

At first built-up on both sides, shortly the buildings peter out on the right. To the left the road follows the course of the River Stour and Bedcote Mill is passed – a skin and rug works. Stambermill railway viaduct approaches. Above, on the right, is Rufford's Fireclay & Brick Works. The viaduct carries the GWR's Oxford, Worcester & Wolverhampton line and also gives access to Stourbridge's locomotive shed. It was built between 20 September 1881 and 14 April 1882, and came into use on 10 May 1882; replacing a Brunel-designed timber one, whose brick supports can still be seen alongside.

Here is the small settlement of Clatterbatch, characterised by fireclay shafts. Settlement is sparse but intensifies after the junctions with Hungary Hill and Bagley Street. This is Stambermill proper and terraced houses are to be seen on each side of the road.

Curving right the line passes the Heart In Hand public house on the right. The tallest part of this used to be a pumping engine house which once drained the nearby Highman's Green Colliery. Passing beneath the lines of the GWR's Stourbridge Extension line both the school (left) and Church of St Mark (right) are passed.

Tucked away between the railway bridge and the church is a small corrugated-iron building which houses a booster station for the tramway's power supply. With housing to the left there is another fire brick and retort works to the right. From here the run to Lye Cross is level and Stourbridge Road is built-up on both sides. There is a passing loop by Rufford Street and another one straddling The Cross and its junction with Pedmore and Dudley roads.

The line up The Lye High Street is single track until just before Christ Church, where there is another passing loop. Next the line passes, on the left, Bank Buildings, the offices of Lye & Wollescote Urban District Council, and on past The Dock, on the left, part of the Lye Waste squatter nail making settlement. There is another passing loop opposite the Unitarian Chapel, which fronts The Dock, and another just past Bromley Street – on the left – alongside Higgins's anvil works. The line then rises to terminate in a passing loop just before the junction of Hayes and Bald's lanes, with, above on the left, The Hayes brickworks and, on the right, a large galvanising works serving the local hollowware industries.

Almost immediately upon opening it was found that it was only with difficulty that a single-deck car could pass under the low railway bridge at Stourbridge. It is likely that the 'Peckham' single deckers, being low built, were the only ones suitable for operating this service. Lye & Wollescote UDC also complained about: 'excessive overcrowding of the cars on the Lye route.' One councillor said: 'It was well known that the cars were constructed to seat twenty-eight, sixteen inside and twelve outside, but he had seen as many as seventy or eighty persons on them.'

There were also problems with the power supply. The D&SDET had to provide an alternative method of bringing a better current supply to The Lye line, the existing one from Hart's Hill, via Stourbridge, was very poor at times of heavy traffic, causing delays to the service. In May 1903, the Company therefore asked Lye & Wollescote UDC for urgent planning approval of a proposed small oil-engined generating station at Stambermill, near Lye. This caused some controversy and the permission was delayed, however, the building was completed by about July 1903, although because of late delivery of its equipment the station was not brought into use until about the end of January, 1904. The equipment included a 160hp diesel oil engine, driving a Brush 6-pole, 100kw generator. This was then fed back into the D&SDET's power system towards the end of 1904 when they laid a connecting cable from Stambermill diesel generating station to Amblecote battery-booster station and a feeder from the latter to the KLR's Kinver Depot.

Stourbridge–The Lye–The Hayes line closed on Saturday, 5 February 1927 and was replaced by Midland Red buses operated by the BMMO.

A very accurate scale model of the kind of tramcar used on the Stourbridge–The Lye line from 1915 onwards, built by the late Eric Jackson-Stevens. They seated 32, in two compartments, and were of a low-roof design because of height restrictions beneath the railway bridge at Stourbridge. *(Author's Collection)*

(Upper) High Street, Stourbridge, with Foster Street and the junction for the Stourbridge–The Lye line on the right. This is a richly detailed image which shows the wide spacing of the High Street tracks and the pattern created by the Jarrah-wood blocks the street was paved with. Cars bound for The Lye had to run up the High Street to more or less the vantage point of the photographer, change direction, and then take the curve into Foster Street. Bordeaux House, on the right, was built by Edward Rutland, a wine importer – hence its name! *(Author's Collection)*

Foster Street East connected Foster Street with Birmingham Street. Here the Stourbridge–The Lye track can be seen in the road. Every March Stourbridge used to have a large annual horse fair, which was held in Foster Street, and is almost certainly what is depicted here. The ten-day fair was described as 'one of the most celebrated horse fairs in the kingdom, which is well supplied and attended by dealers from the continent and all parts.' Doubtless the tramcar motormen negotiated this street with especial care during the horse fair! *(Author's Collection)*

More or less the same location as the previous photograph, but with animals somewhat larger than horses! The date is September 1912 and the most likely reason for elephants being on the loose in Stourbridge is that the circus was in town! *(www.stourbridge.com)*

A view from St John's School, across Foster Street East towards Vauxhall Road, on a snowy winter's day. The Stourbridge–The Lye lines overhead can be seen to good effect. Behind the gas lamp is The Vauxhall Inn and in the distance to the right is St John's Church. It must have been snowing hard as the falling snow has been captured too! *(www.stourbridge.com)*

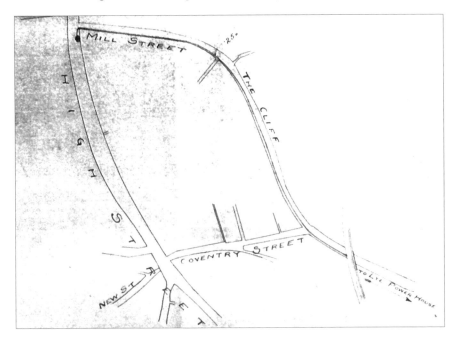

The Stourbridge–The Lye line was one where the power feeder cables did not exactly follow the same route as the tramlines. This construction plan shows that they came from the end of the original Stourbridge terminus at Mill Street and followed both this and Mill Street – today the course of part of Stourbridge's Ring Road – before joining the tramway proper along Birmingham Street – unlabelled, bottom right. *(Author's Collection)*

Birmingham Street, Stourbridge, with the Stourbridge–The Lye line running along the road towards Stambermill Viaduct, seen in the background. This was built in 1881–2 and replaced a timber one – the brick supports of which still remain. Clatterbatch, a small settlement, can be seen through the viaduct's arches, over which a locomotive runs light engine to Stourbridge locomotive shed. *(Author's Collection)*

The Heart in Hand, Stourbridge Road, Stambermill. Both the track and the overhead wires of the Stourbridge–The Lye line can be seen in the bottom and top left-hand corners. David Percival Warr brewed his 'Pure' ales on the premises. The three-storey portion of the building to the left was formerly a pumping engine house which once drained the nearby Highman's Green Colliery – something only discovered when it was demolished! *(Author's Collection)*

The Church of St Mark, Stambermill, which was demolished in February 1986. The Stambermill booster power station was situated between this and the railway bridge off this image to the right. *(Author's Collection)*

This scene at Lye Cross, from Pedmore Road, is very animated, with two policemen and various people pausing to pose for the camera. The house, centre right, belonged to Dr Hardwicke, the local GP. His son – Cedric – became a famous actor and Hollywood star. Above the first person on the left is the bent column of a gas lamp – was this by any chance the one that had to be re-sited to give sufficient clearance for the tramcars? *(Author's Collection)*

The Lye High Street, immediately right of the last image. This is another wonderfully detailed and animated scene, which shows the gradient on the street and the way in which it undulated en route. To the right is the Rose & Crown Hotel, known locally as 'Polly Brookes's', which had a Club Room above, and to the right is The Old Cross Inn, known as 'The Merricks Bar', which forms quite a contrast! The only mechanical vehicle is a bicycle; everything else is horse-drawn. The overhead wiring is impressive, with at least five side arms to view. *(Author's Collection)*

Finally a tramcar – seen working towards the camera on the tracks visible in the previous photograph. Immediately behind the car stand the Centre Buildings, erected around 1900 by wholesale clothing manufacturer Elisha Cartwright, whose factory stood alongside. There were four shops with two-storey houses above. At the same time as the buildings were finished, Elisha had a son, which he named 'Centre'! *(Author's Collection)*

This is as close to The Hayes terminus of the Stourbridge– The Lye line that it is possible to reach in photographs. Here, The Dock is behind the buildings on the left and the tower is from the Unitarian Chapel. The line continued and rose to terminate in a passing loop just before the junction of Hayes and Bald's lanes. *(Author's Collection)*

10

STOURBRIDGE TO WOLLASTON VIA ENVILLE STREET

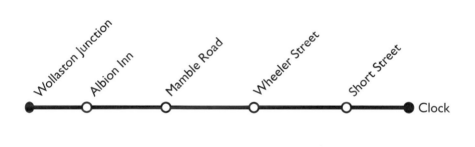

As soon as the KLR opened complaints began to be received from Stourbridge people over the inconvenience they experienced when catching the trams. They had to take a Dudley car to The Fish and change, or walk along Enville Street and Withy Bank into Wollaston. Either way, some effort, or sometimes very long waits, resulted. The tramway company responded by agreeing to build a line connecting Stourbridge with Wollaston along Enville Street and Withy Bank.

Powers to build the line were included in the D&SDET's Dudley & District Light Railways (Extensions) Order, 1900 which was granted its powers on 3 April 1900. These included a line 5 furlongs 7 chains and 1 chain long connecting curves to south and north, respectively, with line No.4 of the 1898 Order, in Stourbridge High Street, then along Enville Street and Bridgnorth Road, to terminate by a junction with the authorised KLR at High Street, Wollaston. The Enville Street line was built in early 1902. By the end of May the track was complete and by early July the traction poles were erected. It opened on 13 December 1902 with a service frequency of one car about every twelve minutes. The line was operated as a shuttle service from Enville

Street to the Wollaston Junction, usually by one single-deck car; through passengers changing there to the Kinver cars.

The line begins at a single-line left-hand junction with the main Dudley–Stourbridge tramway's High Street Extension line just past the junction with Coventry Street and continues as single line for a short length before diverging into a long double-track passing loop, which extends a few yards past Hemplands Road. The line then becomes single. At this point too, the overhead, which had been carried on span wires between pairs of traction poles on both sides of the road, changes to being supported on side arms borne on traction poles on the left-hand side of the road only.

Fare Stage 1 is by Short Street. A second passing loop extends between West and Wheeler streets. Again, the overhead is carried on span wires between pairs of traction poles on both sides of the road, but after the loop it returns to being carried on side arms borne on traction poles on the right-hand side of the road only.

Fare Stage 2 is between Wheeler and Cecil Streets. The line then reverts to single line once more as it runs past Summer Street. To this point the route has passed by rows of terraces, shops and public houses, but past Cecil Street the development on the right-hand side is much sparser.

Beyond Summer Street there are terraces only on the left-hand side, the fields to the right being undeveloped. A third passing loop is situated on the bend in the road before Mamble Road. Fare Stage 3 is just before this loop. Through and beyond the loop the overhead is again carried on span wires between pairs of traction poles on both sides of the road; an arrangement that continues when the line once again becomes single as it passes up Withy Bank. Again, all the development, mainly terraced housing, is on the left-hand side of the road until the Church of Saint James and its school are reached on the right. Fare Stage 4 is part way up Withy Bank, opposite The Albion Inn. A fifth and final passing loop begins by King Street and continues double track to form a junction with the main KLR Fish–Kinver line at Wollaston Junction.

In May 1905, Stourbridge Council decided that, as the double line to The Ridge was now completed, it was time that it insisted on the running of a car through from Enville Street to this point. It was stated that one of the conditions on which the Council approved the doubling of the Kinver line within the Stourbridge boundary, was that a through service from Stourbridge to Kinver should be run when the whole of the line to Kinver was doubled; others were halfpenny fares on the Wollaston line with a penny stage to The Ridge, also through fares from Stourbridge to Kingswinford.

Around 1910–11, a little Brush-built single deck 'Directors' Saloon', originally built for the South Staffordshire Tramways Co. and used in the early years in connection with opening and inspection of new routes, was now transferred to the D&SDET, becoming No. 20. It was fitted with longitudinal seats for twenty passengers, still retaining its elaborate ceiling and panelling, but all other special fittings were removed. This little car was put into normal passenger operation, always working on the Enville Street shuttle service until it was taken out of service about 1913.

Few services were more complained about than the Stourbridge–Wollaston one. On 22 August 1925, Stourbridge Town Council heard complaints about the trams not running in the mornings from Stourbridge and of general dissatisfaction about the tram services. However, the DS&DET were not in the mood to listen as on 24 July 1926 the *Country Express* reported on a 'Tramway Enquiry' which included further discussions regarding the proposed abandonment of the Stourbridge–Wollaston via Enville Street service. The DS&DET put forward the following estimated costs: £4,900 for renewals; £2,400 to replace two tramcars; a total of £7,300 or £245 per year at 4 per cent. Over an eight-month period on the Enville Street line it has been estimated that it had lost about £400 a year, made up of a £200 working loss and a further £200 put by for renewals. Omnibus fares would be approximately a penny per mile for ordinary fares and a halfpenny per mile for working people's fares. In the face of these figures the line was abandoned on Tuesday, 16 November 1926.

This is the only known image showing the junction between the Stourbridge High Street Extension line and the Stourbridge–Wollaston via Enville Street one, seen in the foreground here, swinging right. To the left is Coventry Street, with The Old Bank on the corner and to the right is New Street. In the background is Car No. 23 of 1901. *(History of Wollaston Group)*

Right: The section of Enville Street between West and Wheeler streets is little changed on the left-hand side towards Wollaston. Now, as when the Stourbridge–Wollaston trams ran, the road passes the Royal Exchange Inn, formerly run by Frank Matthews, seen here with his wife. *(History of Wollaston Group)*

Left: Next to the Royal Exchange were North's Butchers and this then all too common sight would have greeted passengers on the Stourbridge–Wollaston line as they passed by. *(History of Wollaston Group)*

Right: Between Cecil and Summer streets stood, and still stands, the Queen's Head Inn, seen here with its dog-owning landlord and faces peering out through the windows. In the foreground a small fragment of the Stourbridge–Wollaston tramlines can be glimpsed. This is the only photograph upon which any track before Wollaston on this line can be seen. *(History of Wollaston Group)*

Fare Stage 4 on the Stourbridge–Wollaston line was part way up Withy Bank, opposite The Albion Inn, seen here. A public house since at least 1841, in the tramway period it was run by the redoubtable Mary Kendrick, pictured here with her family. There is no date for the photograph, but it must pre-date 31 January 1921, when the pub closed down! *(History of Wollaston Group)*

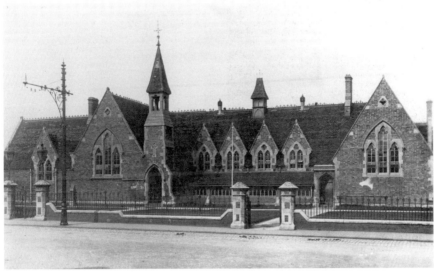

Wollaston Schools, Bridgnorth Road, Wollaston, opened on 28 February 1859 and seen here around 1902. The track and overhead of the Stourbridge–Wollaston line can clearly be seen running left–right across the photograph. By the crispness of the paint on the traction pole it is likely that this was taken at or close to the opening of the line on 13 December 1902. The scrollwork on the supporting brackets to the traction pole side arm is very impressive. *(History of Wollaston Group)*

Wollaston Junction between the KLR (left) and the Stourbridge–Wollaston line (right). KLR car No. 51 is working towards The Fish terminus at Amblecote. This was one of the special open-sided 'toastrack' cars built especially for the KLR and introduced in 1902. Working the Stourbridge service is Car No. 45, delivered in December 1900. This worked on the D&SDET until around 1919 and was used until 1930 as a shunter at the tramway works at Tividale. *(History of Wollaston Group)*

The clearest view of the Stourbridge–Wollaston line comes from this detail from a postcard view of Wollaston Junction. Working the shuttle service that day was Car No. 21, which entered service in November 1900. The photograph must have been taken between 1902 and 1911 as the tramcar was withdrawn from service in the latter year. *(History of Wollaston Group)*

11

OLD HILL TO BLACKHEATH

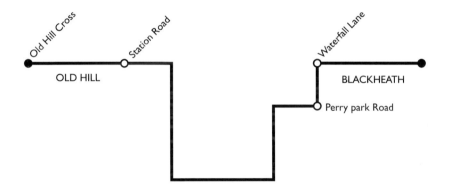

The Old Hill–Blackheath line lay wholly within the Urban District of Rowley Regis. Blackheath stands on a much higher level than Old Hill, there being a difference in height of about 240ft from Old Hill Cross to Blackheath, which had to be overcome in a route length as built of barely 1 ⅞ miles. The narrow and steep Waterfall Lane formed the main connection between the two places, but this was not considered suitable for a tramway. It was proposed that a new road should be built to take the tramway with an easier gradient. Birmingham & Midland Tramways (BMT) Ltd purchased the Blackheath Park Estate, or Tump Estate as it was previously known, and proposals were approved to lay out a new road here, in the form of a deep 'U', or 'double-S', curve to ease the gradient; this new road, known as Perry Park Road, accounted for well over 100ft of the rise. The land not actually required for the tramway road was sold off as building plots, in December 1903.

The contract for the construction of the new road was placed with George Law & Co. and work commenced about March or April, 1903; the Council agreed to the Company's proposal that the track in Perry Park Road should be laid on sleepers, because it was a newly made road on a high embankment and the Board of Trade approval of the plans and specifications was received in September. Unfortunately, work was delayed by Rowley Regis UDC's insistence upon the work being put out to tender, with which the BMT disagreed. They said that they had entered into an agreement with the Council to work the line on lease on specified terms, and it was essential in its own interest that the line should be well built; the Company also pointed out that it had spent a very great deal of money in building the new road, which would be a great boon to the district. It was finally agreed that the Company should submit a formal tender, which the Council eventually accepted in February 1904. Construction commenced in about April or May 1904.

Like the other DS&DET lines, the Old Hill–Blackheath one is single track with passing loops. It begins at a junction with the main Dudley–Cradley Heath line at Reddall Hill Road. It continues along Halesowen Road to Old Hill Cross and through the centre of Old Hill, which is built up on both sides with shops and terraced housing. Past King Street on the left the tramway passes beneath a bridge carrying a mineral railway linking sidings at Cradley Heath Station with Fly Colliery, to the south of Garratt's Lane, which also had basins on the Dudley Canal. Immediately past this to the left is the Zion's Hill Chapel and Sunday school, and to the right Old Hill Police Station, followed by the Church of The Holy Trinity.

The line follows Halesowen Road to its junction with Station Road, then following the latter. Quite quickly it passes under a bridge carrying the GWR's Netherton & Halesowen Branch northwards from its junction at Old Hill Station, which is itself passed next on the right. The direct route to Blackheath would have been up Waterfall Lane, but the tramway company considered this too steep for safe tramway operation. So they constructed a new road – called Perry Park Road after a large house off Waterfall Lane – which raised the tramway over 100ft.

Constructed during 1904, this section of the line was initially devoid of any features, although houses were developed on its left-hand side once the tramway was completed. Perry Park Road connects with Highfield Road, then under development, the line using this and Holly Road to gain High Street. From here it runs straight to its junction with Oldbury Road on the left, which it follows as far as the Handel Hotel at the junction with Birmingham Road, where it terminates.

The Old Hill–Blackheath line opened on Saturday, 19 November 1904. The service was every fifteen or thirty minutes. The route operated until Thursday, 30 June 1927.

Starting point for the majority of the routes from Dudley was the Market Place, by the fountain. Departures were signalled on the board seen in this enlarged view. The clocks were dummies, whose hands could be positioned as required. On this day, at 14.55 a car was due to depart for BRIERLEY HILL, FISH INN for KINVER, STOURBRIDGE, THE LYE; at 15.00 one was due to depart for NETHERTON, OLD HILL AND BLACKHEATH, CRADLEY; and at 15.05 a car would leave for KINGSWINFORD, WORDSLEY, BRETTLE LANE. Note how the words 'NETHERTON, OLD HILL AND BLACKHEATH' have been added later in smaller lettering! *(Author's Collection)*

Car No. 2 swings left out of Reddall Hill Road en route for Dudley with the junction for the Old Hill–Blackheath line on the extreme left. *(Author's Collection)*

Old Hill Cross, towards the end of the working life of the Old Hill–Blackheath line. This is the first passing loop on the line after the junction with the Cradley Heath one at Reddall Hill Road. The flatbed truck and delivery van place this view in the mid-1920s. Collins & Co.'s Grocers & Provision Merchants shop is called 'YE OLDE CROSS STORES' but somehow the painted-on timber framing doesn't quite work! *(Author's Collection)*

A view along Halesowen Road, Old Hill, looking back towards Old Hill Cross. Again, the motorcycle tends to date this at some time during the 1920s. The imposing building on the skyline centre right is Trinity Hall. *(Author's Collection)*

A stunning image showing Perry Park Road nearing completion. The earthworks associated with this are truly impressive and the sleepers on which the track was laid can be seen to good advantage. To the left the Stourbridge Extension railway enters a cutting as it approaches Old Hill Tunnel and the Dudley Canal crosses the centre of the image. Close to both is the wonderfully named Sportsman & Railway Hotel, which can be seen above the fifth traction pole from the left. The chimneys to the left of the railway are from a brickworks and the impressive stack on the right was part of the South Staffordshire Mines Drainage Works. *(Digital Photographic Images)*

A Blackheath-bound tram ascending the lower portion of Perry Park Road. There were no stops on this section of the line and the run was taken in one go. Second only to riding the KLR, this section of the DS&DET's system is probably the one most people would have liked to ride on. Built well within the limits of tramcar traction, people can now drive up the road and few can fail to be impressed with how well the tramcars coped with the curves and gradients. *(Author's Collection)*

The end of the Old Hill–Blackheath line – the terminal stub outside the Handel Hotel in Oldbury Road, Blackheath, photographed during the first half of 1904 as George Law's workers finish off the tramway's overhead. Their wagons are arrayed around the junction of Birmingham Road (left) and Oldbury Road (right). The Handel Hotel was then run by 'A. Smets' and was a North Worcestershire Breweries house. Their breweries were in Stourbridge and at Round Oak near Brierley Hill and were taken over by the Wolverhampton & Dudley Breweries in 1910. *(Author's Collection)*

12

CLOSURE
AND AFTER

With the opening of the Old Hill–Blackheath line on Saturday, 19 November 1904, the DS&DET system reached its greatest extent. This was not the company's original intention. In the early 1900s they had plans to extend their existing lines and to build new ones. These included taking The Lye route through to Halesowen and an even more ambitious idea of linking the KLR with the Kidderminster & Stourport tramway by means of a line via Cookley. However, not everyone liked the tramways and they had a formidable opponent in the form of Isaac Nash – the Chairman of Stourbridge Urban District Council.

A public notice for a meeting of Owners and Ratepayers of Stourbridge to be held at the Town Hall on 23 February 1903, called by Isaac Nash, Chairman of the Council. The purpose of the meeting was to gain sanction to use Council monies to oppose The Dudley, Stourbridge & District Tramways Bill 1903, which would have seen further refinement of the DS&DET system. *(Author's Collection)*

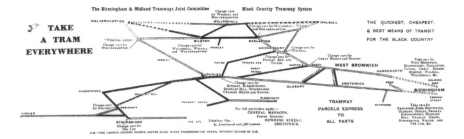

TAKE A TRAM EVERYWHERE was the proud boast of this joint system map which used to be carried on tramcars. This whole system operated for just over twenty-one years between 1904 and 1925, before the system began to contract through line closures. *(Author's Collection)*

It had been Nash who had forced the DS&DET to construct their line through (Upper) High Street Stourbridge the way they had, including the use of Jarrah-wood block paving. He lobbied against the tramway company's plans and organised public meetings in opposition to their 1903 and 1904 Parliamentary bills. The former gained royal assent on 11 August 1903, but the latter foundered because of local opposition. So, the major engineering achievement of constructing Perry Park Road became the DS&DET's last and probably finest achievement.

The DS&DET tramway system operated at its greatest extent for just twenty-one years, one month and twelve days before the first of the line closures described above. In summary these were:

- 31 December 1925: Dudley Station–Kingswinford (Summerhill)
- 10 April 1926: Kingswinford (Summerhill) –Stourbridge
- 16 November 1926: Stourbridge–Wollaston via Enville Street
- 5 February 1927: Stourbridge (Foster Street)–Lye
- 30 June 1927: Old Hill–Blackheath
- 31 December 1929: Dudley Station–Cradley Heath (Five Ways) via Netherton

In addition to these closures, the DS&DET's services did not recover from the company's reaction to the General Strike (4–13 May 1926); thereafter, services never returned to their pre-strike levels and operations were transferred to Tividale, leaving Hart's Hill and Amblecote as unstaffed depots. The Birmingham & Midland Motor Omnibus Company (BMMO), in which the BET held a controlling interest, opened a garage in Stourbridge in 1926. This was at a time when the DS&DET Co. Ltd had financial problems from bus competition and a lack of resources to fund track renewals.

On 14 January 1928, the BMMO began a service between Dudley and Stourbridge in conjunction with the trams. Dudley Corporation owned the tramways and light railways in the borough, which it had leased to the BET for a term of thirty years from 1 January 1909. Although the corporation had no statutory powers, on 10 September 1929 an agreement was entered into between Dudley Corporation, the BMMO and the BET, which, provided that the corporation would take a surrender of the lease of the tramways and light railways within the borough from the BET, on completion of which the BMMO agreed to operate motor buses over the tramway and light railway routes and other bus routes in the borough on behalf of Dudley Corporation, paying it the net profits on all routes within the borough on a proportionate route mileage basis less a charge of 3d (1p) per mile for depreciation and interest. The agreement was for a term of twenty-one years from 1 October 1929.

The D&SDET Co. had a sub-lease from the BET of the Dudley tramways, which was not due to expire until 31 December 1938, but it was agreed that the BMMO would take-over the tramway company's liability under the lease subject to no further competition being permitted at least until 1938.

At the end of January the tramway company wrote to all the Local Authorities in the tramway's area, stating that they wanted to abandon the remaining tramway services as soon as possible. To avoid the need to obtain an order for the purpose, they hoped to reach agreement for closure. Dudley agreed, and terms were soon followed with Stourbridge, Amblecote and Brierley Hill councils. This was all agreed by early February and the main Dudley–Stourbridge route closed on Saturday, 1 March 1930. The last tram was Car No. 23 with Joseph Neath (driver) and John Bloomer (conductor). It left Stourbridge for Dudley at 23.00 on Saturday, 1 March 1930 and travelled as far as Brierley Hill by 23.15 with 26 passengers on board. There was a small farewell ceremony at Five Ways then the car left without any passengers at 23.40 for Tividale depot, where it arrived at 00.15 on 2 March 1930.

Taken on the last day of DS&DET tramway operation – Saturday, 1 March 1930 – this snapshot is sometimes said to be the last tram of all, but that ran after 23.00 that day. This is Car No. 8 outside The Red Lion Inn in High Street, Brierley Hill, earlier in the day; an informal snapshot taken by a local person keen to record the passing of the trams and asked the crew to pose by their car. (Author's Collection)

Until 1939, it was still possible to reach Dudley by tram from the Birmingham direction via services operated by Birmingham Corporation. Two routes served Dudley – the 74 (City–Dudley) and the 87 (City–Oldbury & Dudley). The former route was withdrawn on 1 April 1939 and when, on 30 September 1939, the Corporation's leases on the lines in Smethwick and Dudley expired, nine more tram routes were withdrawn, including the 87. These would be the only Birmingham Corporation tram routes withdrawn during the war. Thereafter, travel to and from Dudley was by bus or, until 1964, rail.

Cars on both of Birmingham Corporation's services to Dudley, photographed in the early months of 1938. Closest to the camera is a car on Route 74, whilst the older open-balcony car is on the 87 Route. Extreme right, the Pickford's office was formerly a ticket office for the DS&DET, where tickets to Kinver could be bought. Behind the trams the steel frame of Dudley Hippodrome is taking shape. This replaced Dudley's Opera House – which was destroyed by fire on 1 November 1936. *(Author's Collection)*

With the Dudley route closures pending, enthusiasts' groups, such as the Light Railway Transport League (LRTL), organised special tours of the threatened lines. Here is Birmingham Corporation's most modern car, No. 843 at Dudley terminus on 23 October 1938 on an LRTL tour which had begun at Rednal. *(W.A. Camwell/Author's Collection)*

From 2 April 1939, Dudley was only served by Birmingham Corporation trams on Route 87. Here is Car No. 153 of 1906 seen at Dudley Station terminus in June 1939. The notices on the windows may have been about the forthcoming withdrawal of the service, which was replaced by Midland Red service B87 on 1 October 1939. *(Peter Glews Collection)*

This view of work to rebuild the frontage of King Edward VI Grammar School in Lower High Street, Stourbridge in 1934 reveals that the tramlines were still in the road and that the traction poles were still standing, converted to use as lamp standards. *(Author's Collection)*

Another view of Lower High Street, Stourbridge, also in the 1930s, again showing both the tramlines and traction poles from the Dudley–Stourbridge line still in situ. The view is towards Amblecote and one of the holders of Stourbridge gasworks. *(Author's Collection)*

Elsewhere, the DS&DET's tramlines were simply buried under generations of road resurfacing. One example was the start of the KLR at The Fish, Amblecote, where the lines lay forgotten for sixty-three years before being unearthed as part of road junction improvements in May 1993. Here contractors puzzle over what to do with them! *(F.T. Gibbs)*

These are the same 'rediscovered' KLR tramlines, removed and piled up on the side of the road at The Fish, Amblecote in May 1993. *(F.T. Gibbs)*

Quite a lot of DS&DET tramlines still remain buried under the local roads only to appear during road and other utility company works. These are in Lower High Street, Stourbridge and were uncovered on 25 August 2006. Fortunately, they were so embedded that the contractors worked around them and they were later covered over. *(Author)*

Also surviving in some places along the former DS&DET lines are the remains of waiting shelters. This one also served as a bus shelter for many years before being partly walled up and turned into a planter. It was photographed on 11 May 1991. *(Author)*

This former tramway waiting shelter is on Birmingham Street, Stourbridge, just before the junction with Hungary Hill. It provided some comfort to passengers using the Stourbridge–The Lye route between 1902 and 1927 and then for bus passengers for some years more. *(Author)*

When this branch of Lloyds Bank was rebuilt in the mid-1920s the two bays on the right were constructed as a tramway waiting shelter. This point was the junction between the Dudley–Cradley Heath and Old Hill–Blackheath lines and was photographed on 11 May 1991. In later years it provided somewhere for the ATM to go. *(Author)*

Foster Street, Stourbridge was the start of the Stourbridge–The Lye route. The DS&DET engineers found it too narrow to erect traction poles to support the overhead wires, so attached them to wall plates called 'rosettes', one of which can be seen on Bordeaux House in Stourbridge sixty-four years after it ceased to have any purpose. *(Author)*

A close up of the tramway overhead 'rosette' seen in the previous photograph. The tube coming out from the centre was for the power feeder cable. *(Author)*

Arguably the most lasting 'remnant' from the DS&DET's tramway lines is Perry Park Road, which raised the tramway over 100ft between Old Hill and Blackheath. It survives in daily use as a public road and is a ready illustration of the curves and gradients that electric tramcars could negotiate with ease. *(Author)*

Two of the DS&DET's standard design of single-decked tramcars have been restored and are used daily at the Black Country Living Museum. The first in service was Car No. 5, which had spent forty years as a garden summerhouse in Dudley. The tramway was inaugurated on 5 August 1980; fifty years after the last DS&DET car had run. *(Author)*

DS&DET Car No. 5 gave twenty-five years' service at the Black Country Living Museum – fifteen more than it had when originally built. The Museum's line is the only narrow gauge electric tramway in the UK. By the mid-1990s, sister Car No. 34 had been restored to take over the service and on 10 September 1996 there was a handover ceremony which provided the rare sight of two DS&DET cars in operation at the same time. As of writing in 2013, Car No. 5 is at the Llangollen Railway for restoration. *(Author)*